10 TEMPTATIONS OF CHURCH

10 TEMPTATIONS OF CHURCH

Why Churches Decline & What to Do About It

John Flowers and Karen Vannoy

ABINGDON PRESS

Nashville

10 TEMPTATIONS OF CHURCH
Why Churches Decline and What To Do About It

Library of Congress Cataloging-in-Publication Data has been requested

ISBN 978-1-4267-4539-3

12 13 14 15 16 17 18 19 20 21—10 9 8 7 6 5 4 3 2 1

MANUFACTURED IN THE UNITED STATES OF AMERICA

Contents

Foreword

The Golden Calf, Bronze Serpent, and Brass Angel

The most beloved passage of Scripture is preceded by one of the most bizarre. In the verses immediately prior to John 3:16, Jesus made a direct comparison between the lifting up of himself on the cross and the lifting up of a brass serpent by Moses toward the end of the wilderness wanderings: "And just as Moses lifted up the serpent in the wilderness, so must the Son of Man be lifted up, that whoever believes in him may have eternal life" (vv. 14-15).

How can the Word-made-flesh, nailed to a cross, be like a serpent-made-bronze, stuck to a stick?

Just before the Hebrews crossed over into the promised land, the Edomites blocked their entrance. The Hebrews had to get creative and take an extended detour around Edom, and they were not happy. Amidst all the complaining and carping about another delay, a plague of stinging serpents set upon the people until Moses interceded directly with God.

Rather than remove the serpents, God instructed Moses to create a bronze replica of what was hurting the people, and elevate it for all to see. Those brave enough to gaze at the brazen serpent were healed. Those who refused to gaze on this gleaming symbol of divine grace and healing power suffered and died (Numbers 21:7-9).

In keeping with human suckiness, those healed came to prefer worshiping the symbol of God's salvation rather than the Savior. They turned an icon into an idol. In a replay of the story of the golden calf, they named the brass serpent Nehushtan, burned incense to the grotesque image, and danced and sang its glory (2 Kings 18:4). Rather than connecting with the Source of their salvation, they preferred to celebrate the symbol of their salvation.

The antidote to the venom was not some magic potion or healing garment or "Open sesame!" The antidote was the willingness of the Hebrew people to face their fears and look straight at the most loathsome thing about them with the eyes of faith. In other words, the curse became the cure. Or, as Paul framed it to the Galatians, "Christ redeemed us from the curse of the law by becoming a curse for us—for it is written, 'Cursed is everyone who hangs on a tree'" (Galatians 3:13).

What is the real meaning of John 3:16 and its bronze serpent background? Look to the truth and live. Hide from the truth and die in the wilderness from the sting of sin and death.

After years of predicting the destruction of Jerusalem and its temple, the Hebrew prophet Ezekiel (whom some scholars believe was the son of Jeremiah) is given a vision of a new temple. He is taken to the top of a high mountain to look over the site of what is to be the new temple (Ezekiel 40–43). His guide is an angel carrying the tools of the construction trade, an angel whose appearance is like brass, with a "line of flax in his hand, and a measuring reed" (Ezekiel 40:3 KJV). As foreman for the construction project, which will require major change and innovation, the brass angel gives some instructions: "Thou son of man, shew the house to the house of Israel, that they may be ashamed of their iniquities: and let them measure the pattern" (Ezekiel 43:10 KJV).

Since the temple no longer exists, "shew the house" means to give the Hebrew people a vision of the temple that connects them to their inglorious past at the same time as it connects them to their higher vision. Only if they connect to the higher vision are they to be shown the forms of the temple, the innovations necessary if the architecture is to be constructed.

> And if they are ashamed of all that they have done, shew them the form of the house, and the fashion thereof, and the goings out thereof, and the comings in thereof, and all the forms thereof, and all the ordinances thereof, and all the forms thereof, and all the laws thereof: and write it in their sight, that they may keep the whole form thereof, and all the ordinances thereof, and do them.
>
> This is the law of the house; Upon the top of the mountain the whole limit thereof round about shall be most holy. Behold, this is the law of the house. (Ezekiel 43:11-12 KJV)

In other words, once the people have been given a vision of their sacred space, they can then be shown what "form" it will take in time, and "laws" can be laid down governing how to get from here to there, how the temple will be built and inhabited. But the vision is not of what is. The vision is not of the status quo. The vision is of the future, of what can be.

The golden calf, the bronze serpent, and the brass angel show us that the status quo is another name for godlessness, and creation is another word for change. To be created is to change. It is the ultimate paradox of human existence: in order for things to stay the same, they have to change. Tradition requires innovation, and vice versa.

If creation is another word for change, there are two essences of creation. The first essence of creation is innovation, and the second essence of creation is separation or differentiation. The book you hold in your hands is a brass angel, carrying in its hands a plumb line and a measuring rod, the two symbols of alteration and innovation.

It is not the strongest of the species that survive, nor the most intelligent, but the ones most responsive to change.

Attributed to Charles Darwin[1]

All innovators have five things in common, according to Jeff Dyer, Hal Gregersen, and Clayto Christensen in *The Innovator's DNA* (2011).[2] These five "discovery skills," also called "habits of mind" by Christensen in earlier works, are associating, questioning, observing, networking, and experimenting. Or to reverse it, where there is no innovation there is the absence of these five "habits of mind." The authors argue further that companies (and churches?) that have the highest "innovation premium" also display these five "discovery skills."

The first "discovery skill" is associating. This means the ability to match unconnected things, to connect the dots, to mix metaphors, to juxtapose difference, to bring opposites into relationship with one another. Associating requires broadening experiences to encounter that which is outside the tradition and tribe, or the mingling, stretching, and breaking of genres as an expressive response to challenges.

Second comes questioning. This means loving questions and asking childlike questions about why things are done like this and not like that, questions that unsettle settled scholarship. This is different from the "questioning" of the Socratic method, which Winston Churchill defined as "giving your friend his head in an argument and progging him into a pit by cunning questions."[3] It is also different from the famous Olympic question once asked by an Asian TV station of a losing athlete: "You are a national disgrace. Please comment."[4]

I was once asked to review a church video where United Methodist church members took to the streets to interview people on why they go to church. One of the questions was "Have you sensed the presence of church in your daily life?" You read that right. Not "Do you sense the presence of God in your daily life?" Not "Have you sensed the presence of Christ in your daily life?" But "Have you sensed the presence of church in your daily life?"

Innovative questioning is like that found in the Book of Job, the book of the Bible in which the most questions are asked. The greatest questioner of all time was Jesus, who was famous for his questions. In fact, if you met Jesus on the street, he was more likely to ask you a question than tell you anything.[5] Innovative questioning reflects an openness to experience, and the extent to which a person is curious, imaginative, questioning, and creative, or conforming, unimaginative, predictable, and uncomfortable with novelty.

Third in the list of "discovery skills" is a talent for observation. Jesus' signature phrase was "Pay Attention." One of the most powerful forces in the universe is self-delusion and denial. In this one phrase, once translated as "Verily, verily I say unto you" or more recently "I tell you the truth" but most accurately "Pay Attention,"[6] Jesus is rebuking our denials and illusions and inviting us to inhabit a state of semiotic awareness in which we see things as they actually are, not as we wish they were.

Some of us have bodies trying to get our attention. Unlike James Joyce's Mr. Duffy, who "lived at a little distance from his body,"[7] many of us live at arm's-length, if not long distance, from our bodies.

When you pay attention to your body, it comes to life.

When you pay attention to your kids, they come to life.

When you pay attention to your spouse, he or she comes to life.

When you pay attention to a plant, it comes to life.

When you pay attention to your church, it comes to life.

Attention is what brings all things to life. Attention is what brings faith to life.

Most important, attention is what brings Christ to life in peoples' lives.

The fourth "discovery skill" is the ability to be a great networker. Innovators hang around, not to cultivate contacts or to grab contracts, but to get ideas and jam over wild and crazy ideas. Great networkers have a connection, not to power structures, but to creative people and communities that prize imagination and change.

The fifth "discovery skill" is constant experimentation. Innovators love to fiddle and conduct spontaneous, serendipitous tests. They also are masters of resourcefulness. When the crowd was so squeezed that a man who needed healing couldn't get through, some friends went up on the roof and lowered him on his mat through the tiles into the middle of the crowd, right in front of Jesus (Luke 5:19). Innovators do not fear to do things differently. Innovators do not fear the change it takes to achieve a destiny. If you can't have a mountaintop experience, have a housetop experience, or even a laptop experience.

The question for every individual and institution is whether he or she or it encourages and rewards these five "discovery skills," or whether these "habits of mind" are beaten down and penalized. John Flowers and Karen Vannoy have written a powerfully revealing and disturbing book that comes at the same issue in a different way. They have conducted a pre-mortem "see for yourself" autopsy on the United Methodist Church and have discovered that it has incentivized decline and stagnation. Or in the framework of "the innovator's DNA," the church is structurally biased against the very habits of mind that would save its future.

What makes this book uplifting and not disheartening is that the authors chart and pave a way forward that is affirming and exciting. They have listened intently to the body's distress call and propose intentional steps that can "break the cycle of fear." In other words, their pre-mortem autopsy lifts up the maladies, bronzing the curse so that it can be cured. They inscribe on that pedestal of wrong prescriptions a hallowed future, no matter how sallow the present or hollow the past. Those who are brave enough to look at their curse are able to be healed. In this way, Flowers and Vannoy have written one of the most hopeful books about the church I have read in the past decade. They show how our golden calves, when they are lifted up as bronze serpents, can summon the brass angels.

Leonard Sweet

E. Stanley Jones Professor at Drew University, Distinguished Visiting Professor at George Fox University, and chief contributor to sermons.com.

Preface

L ocal church decline has been in place since the 1960s and appears to be accelerating in the twenty-first century. The slow death has been charted, not only by each denomination, but also by countless polls, study groups, seminaries, and think tanks. As early as 1993, Benton Johnson, professor of Sociology at the University of Oregon, wrote:

> America's so-called mainline Protestant churches aren't what they used to be. For generations on end, the Methodists, Presbyterians, Congregationalists, Episcopalians, and kindred denominations reported net annual membership gains. As recently as the 1950s their growth rate equaled or exceeded that of the United States as a whole.

> But in the early 1960s their growth slowed down, and after the middle of the decade they had begun to lose members. With very few exceptions, the decline has continued to this date. Never before had any large religious body in this country lost members steadily for so many years. By 1990 these denominations had lost between one-fifth and one-third of the membership they claimed in 1965 and the proportion of Americans affiliated with them had reached a twentieth-century low.[1]

Throughout the decades, pastors and local church leaders have sought to stem the tide of decline, preaching countless sermons, teaching countless classes, and hiring countless consultants to reverse trends and revitalize congregations.

Denominational executives establish committees, task forces, and study groups. Conferences are held, encouragement is given, but privately, everyone knows the sad truth: once they are in its grip, few churches will ever reverse decline. Prevailing wisdom is that money, time, and effort are better spent on starting new congregations, because the old ones seem incapable of rebirth. Listen closely to what might be a familiar story for you as a leader inside your own local congregation:

> Our congregation has been in significant decline for years. The members are committed Christians, and are sad about the membership loss. We acknowledge that something must be done to reverse the decline. Plans are discussed and official votes are taken to make church growth the highest priority. But nothing seems to help and nothing ever changes.

In every church in which we have served, there are good, caring Christians who, more than anything else, want to see their church survive. Take Jerome, for example. He was a charter member of his local church. His house was located two blocks from the land purchased to build their first unit. With other church leaders, he studied blueprints and walked over several times a week to see how the building was going. When it was time for a sanctuary, he raised money to build the new facility. He served in many leadership positions. His wife taught Sunday School. His children grew up in the congregation. But by the late seventies, the church had passed its "heyday." Some thought it was a series of pastors who lacked passion; others thought the city had grown past them to the south and west. Many believed the new generation simply wasn't as faithful as the greatest generation had been. All of these were partial answers to the problems the congregation faced, but just knowing this would never lead them toward solutions. On the one hand, those problems were largely beyond their control. On the other hand, none of the problems identified the one element about which they could actually do something: themselves.

No church member wants to see their local congregation die. It would seem that the motivation to survive would be strong enough to overcome any obstacles. Yet Jerome and those he influenced became a major obstacle in the church's ability to break the forces of decline. In the United States, church after church faces eventual death while helplessly lamenting its fate. What perversity is at work that causes those who sincerely love the church to become obstacles to growth? What are the countervailing forces at work against a church's struggle to be reborn? The gospel can prevail against the gates of hell, but can it prevail against the massive decline facing our congregations?

Like the apostle Paul, churches don't always do the things they want, but instead they do the very thing they hate. Why? While the theological answer is sin at work in us, the organizational answer may just be that members of dying churches unconsciously find a payoff in the church's decline. Albeit at a subconscious level, some members of local churches benefit in some way from the church's shrinking numbers. It is theologically and politically incorrect to oppose church growth, but just beneath the surface, incentives for decline are at work. Unrecognized and unchecked, these incentives for decline form a pattern of behavior that makes growth unlikely and sends churches into a very precarious future.

TEMPTATIONS OF THE LOCAL CHURCH

The church may be the only organization that doesn't exist for the sake of its members. Although individuals in every congregation have needs, the church as body of Christ is in need of no one and nothing except Christ alone. He is our "raison d'être."

Through his power, we are equipped to do every good work in the world, and it is for the salvation of the world that we exist. A church that succumbs to temptations, or becomes defined by the needs of its members, is a "needy" church. Needy churches are about as magnetic as needy people. A church that succumbs to temptation quickly loses its way and forgets its purpose. The needy church is an oxymoron and inevitably spirals into decline.

In the following chapters we look at ten temptations that foster decline. When a congregation begins to structure its common life around these temptations instead of its Christ-given purpose, then the decline of the church becomes an incentive in itself for deeper decline, and the church spirals further away from its true purpose. We will examine what church practices and behaviors are bound up with these needs and incentives, and some ideas for addressing the problems that plague the dying church. There is no doubt that God can still raise up from stones the voices needed to proclaim the good news. What remains to be seen is whether the historic denominations will be among those voices.

PART I
The Need for Power

"Power corrupts and absolute power corrupts absolutely."
—*Lord Acton in a letter, 1887*

Power is a basic need for all human beings, and it may be one of the divinely given aspects of our creation. To have or to need a personal sense of power isn't wrong; it is normal and healthy. When the practice of the local church is tempted to meet this individual need, though, nothing but decline can result.

Power over others, whether institutions or individuals, is intoxicating and therefore addictive. Once you've had it, power is painful to relinquish. This subconscious need could be described like this: "If the decline of my church results in more power flowing my way, I have a strong incentive for that decline to continue." In these next few chapters we will explore this subconscious need and how pastors can respond in a loving and constructive way.

1

The Temptation to Accrue Power

The leadership or nominating committee of any local church is a place where we pastors can do our most productive work. In a best-case scenario, committee members put their heads together, draw their inspiration from the various New Testament listings of spiritual gifts, and pool their knowledge of the membership. They then pray for God's guidance with the firm belief that through spiritual discernment they will be able to identify the right leader for the available church office or ministry. They will weave both new and established leaders together to guide the church as the Holy Spirit directs.

However, in churches filled with members who experience increasing influence as their church grows smaller, the nominating process rarely results in leadership capable of navigating the waters of change. Even when available, new leaders are rarely identified unless they fit into and support the congregation's existing power structures. Most leaders in declining churches have been holding given offices for decades or have rotated through key leadership positions over time. Declining churches resist changing their structure, and their leaders have roles mapped out in order to maintain the church's status quo, even amid decline. If the church was once large, with a complex structure, long-standing leaders typically agree to take on more than one office, rather than reducing congregational structure. Over time, this results in power being compounded by a select group of individuals who hold multiple offices. For example, the finance chairperson also heads the stewardship committee, counts the offering, and is on an additional administrative committee as well. Or the choir member is on the worship committee, the personnel committee, and the church council. The work of ministry becomes reduced to the known circle of leaders. The leaders may feel overworked, burdened, and even burned out, saying, "No one else will do it."

Imagine such a declining church has a sudden spurt of growth, with many new people in attendance. The power equations begin to shift. The responsibilities are shared among many, and the overworked members can take a needed rest, right? If this were to happen, long-time leaders' personal sense of power would decline, which is a "double whammy" of bad news to older adult members of a declining congregation. As they struggle to adapt to feelings of lesser value in society, they face the same prospect of a decreasing role in their church community. If the pastor is the person leading the change, the leaders complain, "The pastor doesn't care about us."

In teaching local church revitalization with pastors and lay leaders, we often ask for and receive a list of current church officers. What follows is a discussion like this:

"I see Bill is listed as a member of the finance committee, memorial committee, and the trustees, and is your head usher. How long has Bill been a member of the finance committee?"

"As long as I can remember."

"What is the defined 'term of office' or length of term for this committee?"

"I don't believe we have a term limitation."

"Why do you keep electing Bill to be a member of the finance committee?"

"Bill is up at the church every time the doors are open. Bill is devoted to the church and he is willing to serve, so we keep electing him. We don't have any folks stepping up for leadership here so we are grateful to Bill. He attends every meeting and he is always willing to share his opinion."

"And the trustees?" we ask. "Bill serves there as well?"

"Yes," one member explains. "He is handy and can fix things. He heads up our spring work day. He calls a couple of his buddies, and they work under his direction all Saturday fixing what needs repair."

"Same story with the memorial committee?" we ask.

"That's right," comes the quick response. "His family has donated all the artwork hanging in our church building. That generosity spans three generations!"

"No different for the ushers?" we assumed.

"Correct again," replied the church member. "It is amazing how much Bill does at this church! He gets all his family members and his friends to serve as ushers. Mostly they hand out bulletins in the back and then visit together until the offering rolls around. Bill is the face of our church; nothing gets past him. It's been that way as long as long as I can remember!"

"And how long has this church been in decline?"

"As long as I can remember," responds one member, who may be making some new connections about what has been happening to her church.

We don't tell this story to question the common belief in this local church that Bill is a Christian saint. He may very well be a deeply disciplined Christian and generous beyond measure with his volunteer time. Church growth will be hard on Bill because the existing situation has produced for him a hidden payoff in decline. It's as if he now has tenure in multiple church roles.

Bill probably started out serving in only one committee office. As the church began to decline, he was asked to serve two offices at the same time. As the decline continued, he was asked to continue serving his offices longer than was customary for this local church. Over time, no new persons came forward who were both gifted and available to serve the offices Bill had occupied for several years.

Eventually Bill picked up the trustee role as well as inheriting the head usher duties once covered by his cousin. As the pond shrank, Bill became a bigger fish. People called him "Mister Methodist." Other members commented, "This place would fall apart without you, Bill." The smaller the church became, the more power, honor, and praise Bill received from his congregation, and the more Bill developed an unspoken personal incentive for the decline to continue.

The polity of many denominations specifies term limits for certain offices. The United Methodist Church requires that trustees, personnel, and nominating committees serve only three years. Many of our churches, though, have one or more members who rotate in and out of these committees. Often in the name of continuity, keeping "institutional memory," and not wanting to hurt anyone's feelings, churches will ignore or circumvent the intention of such term limitations with a conversation like this:

"Carol's term of office ends with the trustees this year, but she told me she'd like to continue. Let's nominate her to a new three-year term."

"That makes sense. Every year since I can remember she has been on the trustees and led the kitchen brigade."

"We used to have all kinds of complaints from women who said the kitchen was filthy after some outside group used it. Carol has put a stop to that!"

"You're right! No one can use the church kitchen now without checking in with her and following the rules she set up. We hardly ever have complaints about the kitchen's availability or about cleanliness!"

Problem solved. Write down Carol's name and move on. Carol will get more accolades for her selfless service and the leadership committee gets to check off the "office now filled" box. Carol enjoys sustaining her strong position of power. Her declining congregation will have an increasing need for her to serve this office and several others in the near future as the local church's labor pool continues to shrink.

Carol is a recently retired bank executive who supervised one hundred employees. She went from a place of power in her business to retirement, and it was a difficult adjustment. Yet retirement offered her the opportunity to do more for her church. She will be ready for other opportunities to supervise others. She thinks, "I am available to serve the Lord wherever and whenever I am needed." As long as her local church cooperates with continuing decline, she'll have plenty to do. Her fellow congregants see her as faithful and selfless, which adds to the reward of doing the same tasks for the church year in and year out.

What incentives does Carol have to participate in behaviors that will grow her church into a thriving congregation? The church may have a mission statement to make new disciples, but there is a personal loss in working such an evangelical purpose, because new leaders carry a double danger. First, their very presence brings less power to established leaders. Second, new people have a pesky way of bringing new ideas—even more so for new converts. New ideas mean even more change, along with loss of recognition and power. Perhaps new people will think the old dishwasher needs replacing and offer to purchase one for the church. But unless Carol agrees, it won't happen. Besides, she's the only one who really knows how to work the old dishwasher and, in her opinion, others just don't understand the machine.

Compounding the problem, once leaders such as Carol find their way into elected church leadership, they will cling tenaciously to that position of power. Some have modest levels of self-awareness and know their leadership skills may be wanting or that they are not appropriately gifted. Yet this position of honor and respect feels good, and the misplaced leader is consequently reluctant, even openly resistant, to giving up the office. Leaders of this type lack the motivation, and sometimes the ability, to reverse the local church decline. Congregational growth will eventually lead to their replacement by someone who has leadership gifts appropriate to the ministry. We don't observe this as a conscious thought process in the church member; it is hidden and operates at a subconscious level.

In a combined sixty years of pastoral ministry, we have seen this dynamic again and again. Here are some examples:

A United Methodist men's president has explosive episodes of rage. This leader takes a group of twenty-five active men down to a group of three.

A United Methodist women's president is elected after six women turned down the nomination. Though there are only a dozen members in attendance, she is unable to conduct a business meeting in less than three and a half hours.

A chairwoman of the evangelism group has zero attendees for her meetings two months in a row. Rather than face difficult questions about her own leadership, she bemoans that women are "no longer committed to the church."

An education chair is unable to carry on an adult conversation.

Occasionally, a brave pastor will tactfully encourage the leader to step down, careful not to hurt anyone's feelings. Yet this is a hard and unrewarding task. No matter how tactfully done, stepping down after a long tenure produces questions, and depending on how the questions are answered, the pastor is often seen as insensitive or controlling. Other long-tenured leaders will be suspicious. To most pastors, it just seems like it isn't worth it. With too many other irons in the fire, it is easier to let it go. So these elected leaders continue to hold offices as the church spirals downward. They all have clear incentives for the continuation of their local church's decline.

LIMIT EVERY MEMBER TO ONE OFFICE

The New Testament is clear that all believers possess gifts that are given to strengthen the body of Christ. It is clear to the most casual church observer that spiritual gifts aren't evenly distributed. Some have many, but everyone has at least one. Consider what is said about spiritual gifts in various Scriptures:

> Now there are varieties of gifts, but the same Spirit; and there are varieties of services, but the same Lord; and there are varieties of activities, but it is the same God who activates all of them in everyone. To each is given a manifestation of the Spirit

for the common good. To one is given through the Spirit the utterance of wisdom, and to another the utterance of knowledge according to the same Spirit, to another faith by the same Sprit, to another gifts of healing by the one Spirit, to another the working of miracles, to another prophecy, to another the discernment of spirits, to another various kinds of tongues, to another the interpretation of tongues. (1 Cor. 12:4-11)

We have gifts that differ according to the grace given to us: prophecy, in proportion to faith; ministry, in ministering; the teacher, in teaching; the exhorter, in exhortation; the giver, in generosity; the leader, in diligence; the compassionate, in cheerfulness. (Romans 12:6-8)

And his gifts were that some should be apostles, some prophets, some evangelists, some pastors and teachers, to equip the saints for the work of ministry, for building up the body of Christ, until we all attain to the unity of the faith and of the knowledge of the Son of God, to mature manhood, to the measure of the stature of the fulness of Christ; so that we may no longer be children, tossed to and fro and carried about with every wind of doctrine, by the cunning of men, by their craftiness in deceitful wiles. Rather, speaking the truth in love, we are to grow up in every way into him who is the head, into Christ, from whom the whole body, joined and knit together by every joint with which it is supplied, when each part is working properly, makes bodily growth and upbuilds itself in love. (Ephesians 4:11-16 RSV)

Now you are the body of Christ and individually members of it. And God has appointed in the church first apostles, second prophets, third teachers, then workers of miracles, then healers, helpers, administrators, speakers in various kinds of tongues. Are all apostles? Are all prophets? Are all teachers? Do all work miracles? Do all possess gifts of healing? Do all speak with tongues? Do all interpret? (1 Cor. 12:27-30 RSV)

Even though one person might have four or five gifts, she doesn't have the time to exercise all of them at once. Or, a church member could clearly have certain gifts, but he is not in a stage of faith development that allows him to hear and respond to God's call.

CLARIFY THE NOMINATING PROCESS

Three factors seem to cloud the leadership nomination process in declining churches. It is evident from the various listings of spiritual gifts that these gifts take many forms, and that some of these are gifts of supporting, financing, and encouraging the leadership of others.

1. Some People Have Support Gifts.

They don't have the gifts needed to recruit, motivate, and activate others. Those with support gifts are naturals at volunteering or agreeing to serve as a leader, even if they don't have the gifts needed. This is because they want to help! That is their gift— their willingness to say yes and support others. Too many nominations to church office are made as a reward for faithful service or because the potential nominee is a friend. Sometimes a nomination is made simply because the nominee is a nice lady, a gentle woman, and everyone likes her.

Couple this with a nominating committee comprised primarily of long-term members who have limited contact with new persons. They begin with a small pool of persons from which to select. They go easily and immediately to those who have helped them in the past with church activities.

We recommend that prior to the first leadership committee meeting, the local church advertise the nomination process via bulletin insert, allowing persons to self-nominate. The ad might read like this:

"Where do you feel God is calling you to leadership? Would you like for the local church to ask you to serve in a program ministry or church office? Where would you like to serve?" Each church should construct this insert to fit their particular needs, taking care to explain clearly the work of each area. Define the office according to what is currently needed for the church, not just to maintain what has always been done. Compile these self-nominations into a working list for the committee.

This is a more transparent process. If you want to serve, then write your name down to request it. This process eliminates people being coy about their desire to serve. This process communicates openness to new leadership. In this process, the leadership committee will identify some surprises in the self-nomination process. Often when we use this process, someone says, "I would never have thought Ruth would have any interest in that position."

It is critical that everyone who turns in a nomination request form be contacted when the proposed slate for office has been completed. This informs those who were nominated that their name will be presented before the church body for election, but more important, to inform others that they weren't nominated to their desired office. Let these folks know reason(s) why, such as:

"We had seventeen people wanting to serve and only three slots open."

"We needed to get some young adults involved in that area."

"We needed your gifts much more in another area of ministry."

Without divulging confidential conversations from the leadership committee deliberations, be honest and straightforward with your feedback. We must learn to speak the truth in love.

2. Too Much Responsibility in Too Many Church Offices Will Take More Time Than One Person Has Available.

Though someone may possess seven distinctive gifts, and even though one of those gifts might be juggling a schedule that you or I would find unmanageable, there are only twenty-four hours in any day.

One and a half hours into a staff parish relations committee meeting, the chairperson offered up this option: "I want to interrupt the conversation at this point and do a 'time check.' I know we said this meeting would last no more than ninety minutes and we are getting close to that time. With everyone's permission, I propose that we plow on through and we should be out of here by nine. Are there any objections?"

A round of muffled "all right by me," "I'm OK with that," and "fine" went around the conference table. Then the pastor said, "I'm not OK with it." All the committee members seemed to be confused. The chair of the committee was a strong layman who possessed more spiritual gifts than many pastors have! He was also serving in three different church positions and one judicatory position. The pastor continued,

"It is eight thirty and you have two small children at home who are just now, I suspect, being readied for bed. If you leave now, you will be able to kiss them goodnight and tuck them into bed. If you are lucky, you will have a moment or two to hear them tell you about their day. I know that three other members of this committee have school-age children at home. They are in the same boat. It is time to go home. We will simply put those things yet to be covered on next month's agenda."

Each person nodded in agreement, shared a prayer, and all set out for home.

One week later the staff parish relations chair came into the church office and said,

"I heard what you said the other night, and I have come to a decision. I love my church, but this is too much. I will stay on as staff parish relations chair, but I am resigning my two other church offices. When I am gone from home two or three evenings each week, it is impossible to be the daddy I want to be to my girls. I hope you understand."

I hope we all understand. If done correctly, effectively serving multiple church offices takes too much time, and the personal costs are enormous. The key phrase is: "serving multiple church offices effectively." No one, not even a ten-gift person, can effectively serve in multiple offices. Between work, family, civic responsibilities, self-care, and church, someone or some commitment will suffer from neglect. Just because a leader agrees to serve in multiple church offices doesn't mean it's effective for the church. Predictably, the church leader will shortchange one or more of those offices either through limited time or energy. The focus won't be there.

These leaders are smart people. They know their job performance in one or more places is inadequate to the task, but being the responsible people they are, having accepted responsibility and not wanting to be quitters, they keep plowing through. Here are some sample responses from these members:

"I said I would do the job, so I'll do it!"

"I can't leave them high and dry for the year!"

"The leadership committee begged me to say yes. I was recruited with the understanding that there was no one else who could fill this slot."

One possible result is embarrassment, guilt, and resentment because of the church leader's inability to do all of these jobs in the same calendar year. Let's purge church life of guilt and embarrassment as potential motivators. Those methods don't work well

14

anyway. If we see that someone is spread too thin to do an effective job, we should check in with him or her. Here's a model of how that conversation might sound:

"How is it going?"

"Things are good, thanks for asking."

"I noticed that you haven't been to the last three trustees meetings, and I was wondering what that was about?"

"I know, and I feel bad about missing, but work has been a hassle and the kids are involved in a lot of school activities. We've been out of town some too. I'm really sorry; I'll try harder."

"That would be great," the pastor answers, "but I want you to think about another possibility. Maybe you are trying to do too much. I know you love this church and care about the facilities, but maybe, with everything else you have going on, it is too much to be a member of the trustees right now. I'm not saying this is the case, but this might be God's way of saying, 'You need to cut back for now.' "

"But I don't want to leave the church in a tough spot!"

"Not to worry," the pastor reassures him. "If God is saying 'not right now' for your service to the church on the trustees, then we need to trust that God is grooming someone else to take that slot. Think about it, pray about it, and let me know in a couple of days. The leadership committee will find a solution."

We must find ways to let people off the hook without guilt and in the context of discerning God's call for their lives.

3. To Answer God's Call and Offer Our Gifts Requires Us to Be at a Certain Stage of Faith Development.

Some persons in the church have leadership gifts but aren't at a stage in their faith where they can or will devote themselves to the task. The worst example of this is when people are nominated to serve in leadership of the local church simply in order to reactivate their involvement. They haven't been around for a while, so the rationale becomes: if they have a job, they will become more regular in their attendance.

It is problematic to use this as a basis for selecting leaders in the church. Nominating leaders with sporadic church attendance patterns will only result in more problems for that local church. They aren't ready for spiritual leadership, as evidenced by their lack of presence. If someone isn't fulfilling the basic vows of church membership, she or he isn't ready for leadership. Sometimes we see people who, in their work or community, are excellent leaders with a lot of charisma, so we reason they would be good at church leadership too. If only they would bring those gifts to bear for the church! Yet if they aren't present regularly with the body, they aren't going to be the kind of leaders the church needs. Leading a civic group may be just a function of a natural gift, but without a passion for the cause, the leader won't be very successful. The same is true of the church. A leader with needed gifts must be passionately willing to use those gifts for the cause of God.

Even if all officers have leadership gifts appropriate to the task, and even if they have time to serve several different offices, this will result in fewer members involved in ministry. "The few" are doing it so well that others aren't needed. The busiest members of the congregation will be relieved; the gifted but uninterested will be relieved. Meanwhile, the newcomer will find the church hard to "break into"; the new members will be reluctant to voice new ideas because—they're new!

Many declining congregations struggle with defining expectations and accountability for their leaders. We have faced that problem at every church in which we have served. In our last two appointments, we worked with our leadership committee to address this need. After one full year of deliberations, conversation, prayer, and tweaking, we came up with a "leadership covenant."

This covenant contains the expectations for leaders in the local church. They aren't rules or a new form of legalism. It is a covenant between God, the leader, and the local church as a whole. We placed the covenant before the general church administrative/programming body, which added a few minor changes. Eventually, it was adopted. From the covenant, we developed a self-assessment form so leaders could see how they were doing. We began to use it in our own annual leadership training events as well. The second year we added a "covenant of respect" to the leadership covenant.

Our leadership covenant and covenant of respect can be found in the appendix, but every community of faith is different. We offer this covenant in order that you might develop your own covenant within your nominating and leadership bodies. Though the implementation takes time, the process itself is identity-forming for the leadership and well worth the time it takes.

The conversation begins simply: "What does it take to be a leader at our church?" Don't even try to answer this alone—it's a question for the body of Christ. Call a meeting of the nominating committee or place the item on the church council agenda. Brainstorm! Encourage creativity. Ask your staff members. Look at it from every angle. We came up with a very long list and then condensed the list into a manageable number of qualities. Find the process that works for you. Be sure to focus on the need for the church to own its clearly defined leadership expectation.

CHAPTER TWO

The Temptation to Exercise Financial Influence

All churches have anxiety about finances. Churches, as well as other nonprofits, struggle to underwrite ministry and local church budgets. Money anxieties are usually greater with churches that have experienced a decade or more of decline. One reason is that a general atmosphere of anxiety or depression pervades declining churches, and it leaks everywhere. Another is that many declining churches haven't been able to grow their churches for so long they have lost faith in their ability to succeed at anything, much less a financial drive.

We are familiar with one church that depends on one person to underwrite forty percent of that church's annual budget. The gentleman is in his late seventies. Ten years earlier, he gave a seven-figure gift to the congregation for a new pipe organ. His power would be enormous under any circumstances, but in a long-suffering, dying congregation, his power is even greater. As the total dollars in this local church's budget have shrunk over the years, his dollar contribution has remained the same. Every year he underwrites a larger percentage of his local church's budget than he did the year before. As the church shrinks, his power increases. With each passing year the governing board is more anxious and more ready to do whatever it takes to keep him happy. He has a strong incentive in place for church decline.

One local church in serious decline has a history of reaching the end of the calendar year short of paying out their denomination's benevolence requests and other end-of-the-year obligations. Their end-of-the-year ritual begins when members of the finance committee gather together, wring their hands, and compose their desperate "end-of-the-year letter." That end-of-the-year letter is hand delivered to three or four patriarchs in the congregation. There is no surprise:

"Ralph, we're trying to finish our budget for the year in the black, and we need your help."

"I know we are behind, and if you remember, I predicted this when the Church Council took unwise risks in putting this budget together in the first place," he scolded.

"True enough, Ralph," said the messenger with some contrition. "We didn't meet our goal."

"And now you want me to bail you out," Ralph pressed his advantage.

"We're just asking for your help," the messenger continued, trying to maintain dignity and self-respect, while knowing how critical Ralph's contribution would be. "Whatever you can do would be greatly appreciated."

Ralph sits the messenger in the chair and makes him wait while Ralph hunts for the missing checkbook.

As he sits down to write the check the congregation badly needs to end the year with a balanced budget, Ralph makes sure to get in one last admonishment to the messenger: "I hope the church will learn from this and be more practical in expenditures for this next year."

Representing the local church and receiving the scolding a parent would give to an irresponsible adult child, the messenger leaves with his bailout contribution. The whole group is grateful for Ralph and buys into his pronouncement of their irresponsibility.

Over time Ralph joins the finance committee for this end-of-the-year calculation and scolding. One year they gathered, facing what they thought was the same dilemma. This time, however, they had one new (and very brave) member. She suggested they try something different and offered to head it up. She proposed that this time, individual members of the finance committee would contact two separate groups of members: those who had joined the church during the last twelve months, and any who had not fulfilled their pledges. Contrary to their history and everyone's expectations, this worked. The local church ended that year in the black.

At the next meeting of the finance committee, everyone around the table sang the doxology. The church administrator said,

"In all my years doing this job, this is the first time we have finished with a balanced budget at year's end. This is incredible!" Backslapping and smiles erupted all around, except from Ralph. For some reason he looked lost.

"We can't let the people know that we have paid all our bills this early," Ralph warned.

"I think we ought to announce it in worship and the newsletter," said another member. "The people need to take this opportunity to celebrate."

"I don't agree! I move that we still send out our end-of-the-year letter," Ralph motioned.

"Didn't you hear, Ralph?" answered a jubilant chair. "We got what we need."

"But some might not have been able to give their expected end-of-the-year gift," Ralph explained.

"Some people wait until the last minute, or until they know what we need."

"Who are we talking about?" asked the chair.

"Well, me for one," Ralph confessed. "I haven't given my end-of-the-year gift yet."

It was a new day. This was the first year in nearly two decades that Ralph and his checkbook weren't needed to bail out church finances. Ralph looked like he was lost, and indeed, he had lost some of his substantial power. The church was not utterly dependent on his bail-out this year. He could only hope his place of personal power would return in future years.

One action like this doesn't stop a church's decline, but it does address a basic incentive for decline. There was a new hope and belief that the body of Christ, rather than an individual member or small group of members, could come together and collectively meet the church's financial needs.

In virtually all declining churches, someone says something like this:

"We need to remember who pays the bills around here."

"I have been a contributing member of this church for over thirty years!"

"I am a long-time member of this church. My parents met and married at this church. My brother, sister, and I were baptized and confirmed in this church."

"Our family gave the (fill in the blank here) to this church so it is hard to believe that you would not honor our current request!"

Generally, these are admonishments directed at pastors or current church leaders. They are usually the protestations of persons who believe they are entitled to have a greater say than others in the church due to their longevity in membership or abundance of giving. Although an understandable human response, there is no place in the church for such feelings of entitlement. Entitlement in our churches not only runs contrary to the gospel, it is an incentive for decline. Feelings of entitlement may be accompanied not only by the threat to withdraw financial support, but the threat to leave the church altogether, which increases the free-floating anxiety prevalent in declining churches.

For pastors and church leaders who have endured years of emptying pews due to death and transfer, the anxiety of yet another withdrawal might be too much to bear. The impulse is to work even harder to keep pew-sitters in place and keep them happy. If we fall victim to this unexamined, anxious response, then we allow those who have personal incentives for the church's decline to dictate local church decisions, and the dysfunctional behavior spreads.

The basic core gospel mandate, "Go therefore and make disciples of all nations" (Matthew 28:19), cannot flourish when we are held hostage by church members, no matter how well-meaning. Vision for growth will first be questioned, then devalued or demoted. Growth isn't simply more church members. Growth means more disciples, more followers of Christ, and assimilation of others into the full life of the Christian community. New leadership voices mean that the voice of long-term members will be mixed with other voices that don't share their history or priorities. As one savvy lay leader said, "The problem with new people is they always bring new ideas. Imagine that!" The strength of new members isn't only that we meet the gospel imperative, but also that new members and their ideas help us adapt to a changing culture.

Basically, we have not stood up to this pressure. Our mainline denominations are shrinking every year. Will our denominational leaders understand that our local church may first shrink in attendance and membership as we put an overall plan of revitalization and growth in place? Will the denominational leaders exercise the necessary patience and cutbacks to weather the onslaught of criticism from those who receive personal benefit and affirmation as a result of continued decline?

Some denominational leaders choose to keep the peace rather than advance the vision. They might say they want both, but they know that is often not possible, as pastoral leaders are often valued by how well they can keep church members happy. One particularly anxious bishop spoke his concern directly to us: "In the last five years, I have gotten more calls and complaints from members of the congregation you two serve than from all the other churches of the conference combined."

We respectfully reminded him that we had only been serving that church for two of those five years! He seemed surprised to realize that the church's complaints were the same no matter who their pastor was. This illustrates just how hard the work of revitalization can be, on denominational leaders as well as pastors. When a grand old church goes into decline, the denomination will, at first, continue to draw on it as if it were the ship of state it used to be. In the United Methodist Church, the denomination depends on the financial support of these once-large bodies. Their choices are:

- Continue to allow the inevitable but slow death produced by the incentives for decline. The ship won't crash until long after their tenure.

- Experience the sharper drop that implementing needed changes can produce, knowing the groundwork is being laid for future growth.

These are unpleasant choices. As a denominational leader I would say, "No! Show me another way!" If you read the literature today on declining churches, you will see that there are no magic bullets. Reversing incentives for decline will require support not only from old members and new potential members of our local church but also from denominational leadership.

KILL ENTITLEMENT CULTURE

At least annually, conduct a church-wide, formal stewardship campaign.

Build expectations around percentage giving. Never practiced percentage giving before? Start with two or three percent with a goal to achieve a tithe within a ten-year period of time. Begin with the pastor and staff, extend to the leadership, and branch out to the congregation.

Thank all your major donors. Their substantial gifts are a generous response to God's call.

Clif Christopher's book, *Not Your Parents' Offering Plate* (Abingdon, 2008), offers more quality, in-depth advice on how to practice effective financial stewardship inside all congregations. Use this or another of the many quality resources about money. Have your finance committee read and study these proven principles together.

The bottom line is that the refusal to be held hostage by those who have benefited from the local church's decline over the years might mean that budgets will have to get tighter before real change takes place. One successful revitalization pastor was asked, "What is the most important ability a revitalization pastor must have in order to bring about necessary change in a congregation?"

"You must be willing to watch money walk out the door," he answered. "One Sunday I watched $100,000 walk out the door. That was the day we went from a church of persons of entitlement to a congregation committed to making disciples for Jesus Christ."

FOUNDATIONS AND ENDOWMENTS

One church we served was full of persons who had benefitted from decades of decline. The president of the local church foundation refused to allow us, the pastors, access to source documents, which defined how designated contributions should be allocated. He had interpreted all the instructions for us, and kept some of the files at home "for safety." The local church foundation had been established two decades before our arrival. The foundation contributions, earned interest income, amounted to thirty percent of the local church's annual budget. We wanted to know what funds were undesignated, what funds were designated for specific purposes, and how the source documents defined those designations. We made a request to view the foundation's source documents over the phone. We made the request face-to-face. We "checked in" with him and asked, "How is that request coming?"

"I'll get on it first thing this next week," he responded. By the end of the next week, we had no documents. When he finally produced the files from home, we discovered some of the documents were kept at the church in a locked file cabinet. You guessed it! Only he had the key.

"Misplaced the key to that file; no need to worry," he said. "It will show up." Another week passed, and still no progress. As the foundation president felt mounting pressure for transparency, he said, "You two take care of the preaching and visiting the hospitals, and we'll take care of the finances."

Let's be clear. The foundation president loved the church. He served the church in many elected offices, and he was a generous contributor to the church's finances. But it was a painful scene when he delivered the paperwork he had stored at home and that precious key to the file cabinet at the church. We didn't expect to find, and we didn't find, any misappropriation of funds. He was an honest man and exercised appropriate fiduciary responsibility with those monies, but transparency meant a reduction in his personal power as a financial leader.

On another occasion, we asked for some monies from the foundation to be spent on something needed in our operating budget.

"Oh, no," he warned. "Those are designated funds with a specific purpose outlined by the donor." After looking at the source documents for the funds in question, we saw that the designation on these funds was for the general operating budget of the church. Maybe he had simply forgotten; maybe it was intentional. It doesn't really matter. The only way this saint of the church had been able to hold on to his power and influence was to cooperate with thirty years of decline and live as if nothing had changed. These aren't people who look with excitement at revitalization possibilities. These are people who lose much of what they value if revitalization takes hold. They clearly have an incentive to keep decline in place.

Anxiety, secrecy, and power cripple the church's stewardship process. If a church has a foundation or endowment, put several steps in place:

In a group of foundation leaders, re-examine the stated purpose of the foundation as recorded in the original document submitted to state authorities. If the recorded document says something like, "The foundation exists for the ministry of First Church," then display the vision, purpose, and journey of the First Church at all foundation meetings.

Do an annual inventory of all source documents to insure the funds are allocated as intended. Try to match existing ministry needs with designated (restricted) funds.

Note undesignated monies for allocation to making disciples for Jesus Christ in order to transform the world. Have all allocation requests pass this or a similar test before funding.

Practice transparency. This is critical to building and maintaining trust between foundation members and the congregation.

Make sure the local church understands that foundations must practice due diligence in proper fiduciary responsibilities, but the governing body (church council, board of elders, deacons, and so on) has the primary function of determining the ministry of the church. Too often, money drives ministry rather than the other way around.

CHAPTER THREE

The Temptation to Gather Information

One declining church had a member who had served as church council secretary for twenty-five years. She was called and told that the nominating committee was trying to bring new people into leadership. She was asked where else in the church she would like to serve after so long a tenure as secretary. She was so angry that she refused to serve another office. Five years later, she still complained to anyone who would listen that she had been ousted from her office. Her constant complaint about the church was, "I never know what's happening anymore. Decisions are made, like changing the doxology, and I am never consulted." Clearly she couldn't adjust to the loss of power. Her efforts were blatant, but often the "information is power" dynamic is practiced more subtly.

In one revitalization assignment we met a couple who never missed a Sunday. During the "church school" hour, this couple parked on the church front lawn, serving cookies. Their cookie ministry was an independent effort. It wasn't connected to the local church structures in any way. The couple purchased the cookies and was dependable in their presence and friendly in their contacts. Their presentation was warm and winning.

This central location, on the local church front lawn, was the traffic pattern for most of those attending church on Sunday mornings. Some folks made a point to stop by each Sunday and catch up on the latest news and gossip. New persons felt welcomed. Still there was a problem. In their eyes, this was a critical ministry and they were providing a selfless service to the local church. But no one else was invited to participate. No one else was invited to serve. They discontinued the practice every summer because they were gone. Besides, it was too hot, they said. When we offered to help recruit people who could carry on the ministry in the summer, they seemed offended. That was a sure sign we had a problem. We hoped our offer to extend the ministry would be seen as validation for their vital ministry, but that wasn't the case.

There is a reason why scripture says, "It is more blessed to give than to receive" (Acts 20:35). It feels good to be the giver of gifts to others, rather than the receiver. When we keep the blessing of giving to ourselves, and fail to allow new persons to experience the blessing of giving of their time, talents, gifts, service, and witness, then we are blocking the chance for new persons to be a blessing to others. As a west Texas preacher used to say, it isn't right to "hog the blessing."

We approached the couple positively. "Will and Nancy, it is great that you have established this refreshment center on the front lawn every Sunday morning."

"We love our church," they said, words of modesty pouring from their mouths. "It is no trouble; we love doing it."

"Have you ever thought of including others in this effort, so it isn't only on you two?" John asked.

"What do you mean?" Nancy asked, apparently confused by the question.

"What we mean is, have you ever thought about developing and leading a team of people to do this ministry?" Karen answered, looking for a light of recognition to turn on or at least some curiosity, neither of which showed on their faces. "You know," John continued, "recruit at least four other couples to each take a Sunday of welcoming at your table. You could do it every fourth or fifth Sunday while others have a chance to be agents of radical hospitality on the remaining Sundays."

"That's not necessary," Will quickly replied. "We don't mind doing it ourselves. We look forward to it."

"That's what I'm saying; maybe you can spread the blessing around and others with similar gifts would be able to serve some Sundays."

Will's voice took on an edge. "Do you want us to quit doing this?"

"No, no, nothing like that," Karen answered.

"Because we pay for everything out of our own pockets. We have never asked for any reimbursement from the church." Will became angrier as he spoke.

"You do a great job. We want you both to continue," we explained, trying to recover. "We were hoping that you would move to a more supervisory and training role. We need you in leadership. Imagine the excitement of empowering others for ministry. You two are perfect persons to model how this radical hospitality should be done. You are warm, energetic, and winning. You could teach others, who might have raw gifts in this area, how to do it correctly. You could design the new system and establish benchmarks to help others be successful. Don't you think it is our job as leaders to empower others for ministry rather than do the hands-on ministry ourselves?"

"Although we have done this for over ten years, we can see you do not support our efforts here," Will cut us off. "We'll have to think about what you have said."

At that point, our conversation was over. Apparently there was no room for anyone else to share in this ministry that Will and Nancy had claimed for their own. From their perch at that refreshments table, they were "communication central." They knew everything that was going on before anyone else. Will and Nancy were not open to bringing others into this exclusive ministry, but it wasn't because they felt rejected. They had full, rich lives with responsibilities, status, many social activities, and their family. For them to include new people would cut off access to a major information station. Less information means less power. They are tempted by the power of information. To keep exclusive rights to this radical hospitality station kept their power in place and denied an opportunity for others to serve and grow.

Ironically, church growth would validate their hospitality, which would bring great recognition to them. But not as much recognition as they were receiving in their current setup:

"Thank you, Will and Nancy, for your faithfulness every Sunday at this hospitality station."

"Thank you, Will and Nancy, for your extra-mile offerings to the church in the form of cookies."

"Thank you, Will and Nancy, for being the ones who care about making others feel welcome."

"I don't know what we would do without Will and Nancy's dedication."

The desperation of the pastor and lay leadership to do whatever it takes to keep Will and Nancy happy and in place is palpable. Are they indispensable? It would appear so, as the church continues to decline, and there are fewer and fewer volunteer workers available to the congregation.

It is fearful to any congregation member, but especially a new member, to move into a leadership role that the outgoing leader didn't want to give up. To avoid this, at the opposite end of the church's campus, the church's hospitality committee set up an additional welcome center that was open after the last worship service. Will and Nancy were so offended they gave up their hospitality station in less than a year. For Will and Nancy, the new welcome center became not the hoped for symbol of a wider and deeper hospitality but a symbol of their rejection. They began to see other new leaders and new ministry efforts as a rejection of the local church's history and traditions. Since the two were long-term members with powerful personalities, they easily intimidated others by voicing their displeasure. Few were willing to take them on.

When information is used as power, it isn't necessarily limited to one person or family. Longtime members' knowledge of the history of a church (whether accurate or not) can be wielded in a manner that crushes the best laid plans. The Wills and Nancys of congregational life will find easy allies in other long-term members, allies like Hazel.

She was the local church matriarch and carried the church's corporate history in her memory. She attended meetings whether she was on the committee or not, because she liked to stay "in the know." She knew the history of every ministry tactic and presumably the tastes of the congregation in general. Many members affirmed her presence: "Oh, you want Hazel in the meetings. She knows everything about . . . (fill in the blank: the kitchen, the sanctuary, the parlor, and the children's rooms)."

Hazel dropped in on one meeting after hearing of a discussion about the walls outside the children's rooms. One artistic new member was very excited about some wall murals she had seen and wanted to duplicate the concept for the church. She had drawn up some sketches and submitted them to the committee for discussion. Her enthusiasm was catching, and the whole group was bubbling over with excitement. Hazel casually entered the room.

"Wow, what's going on here? You sound excited," Hazel said with a big smile.

"Hi, Hazel! Come on in! We're discussing painting murals on the walls outside the children's classrooms," the chairperson said, and handed Hazel some drawings Miriam had drafted.

A slight scowl crossed Hazel's face. She said, "Oh, I don't think this is a good idea at all. It doesn't complement our buildings or architecture, or really even the church's overall style. Who drew these?"

The group became quiet as a flushed Miriam said, "I did. I saw them at another church and thought they were beautiful. I'm sorry you don't like them."

The committee held its collective breath as Hazel said softly but firmly, "I'm sorry, dear. I don't mean to hurt your feelings. They are lovely but inappropriate for here. I am not in favor of this at all."

The group squirmed uncomfortably. The pastor finally said, "Hazel, I believe others think differently than you do, but thank you for sharing with us your concerns."

Hazel's mouth gently dropped open and a look of complete surprise came over her face. It had never crossed Hazel's mind that someone might not share her opinion. No one in the church had ever before questioned her impeccable sense of propriety.

CHANGE THE WAY LEADERS INTERACT WITH THOSE INCENTIVIZED FOR DECLINE

Contrast these three members with Paul, the newly elected head usher. He had been asked to take over for Maxine, who had been the first woman head usher, a job that was treated as a tenured position in that church. Though she was getting too old to do the job, she also couldn't seem to give it up. Paul used his leadership gifts to keep Maxine involved in the task of ushering. Paul had little need for power in the church, and if Maxine wanted to make a decision, he usually let her do so. If she began to criticize others, though, or attempt to subvert new efforts to reach others and welcome them through worship, he would gently say, "Oh, we can give this new way a try, can't we? Let's let our young people and new members guide us in this area." Gradually, Maxine was delighted to "have Paul's help."

Members like Will, Nancy, and Maxine are used to having their way. You cannot change that about them. But you can make sure all your leaders are trained at the kind of intervention that the pastor did with Maxine. It isn't true that people like that must continue to hold the congregation back. It is true that they aren't capable of regulating themselves. Someone else must be willing to say to them kindly but clearly, "Thank you. We care about you. We aren't going to do it your way." Most of the congregation just wants to know what's going on before it happens. The few who want to control the outcome may become so frustrated that they end up leaving the church. Again, you can't change that. But you can establish the boundaries of acceptable behavior.

COMMUNICATE IN AS
MANY FORMS AS POSSIBLE

If we want young adults among our first-time and repeat visitors, we must do things online. Websites, online newsletters, email, social networking, and prayer cards submitted during worship are "in." These are new communication pathways available to every local church. Armed with aggressive pursuit skills, we increase our chances for success. Among young adults, eighty percent of those who visit a church for the first time have looked at the church's website on the Internet prior to attending. Young adults want to first connect with the website.

All young adults are different. There is one local church website that represents itself as a small church in the middle of the city. The website says, using a familiar television show slogan, "If you are a small town person at heart, brought to the city for school or work, and you miss your small church from home, we are the place where everybody knows your name and they're always glad you came." This small church is marketing from its strength. Lots of multigenerational ministries are going on in the congregation.

Well-designed and updated websites are a large part of a young adult's world. They don't watch much TV but surf the Web four to five hours a day. They want to be a part of a church that understands them, and that means a church that understands how the Web plays a part in their life. Remember the marketing phrase, "No one gets a second chance to make a first impression?" The first impression used to begin for first-time visitors at the door of the sanctuary on Sunday morning. This is no longer the case. The first-time visit is often online. Saturday night's peek at your church's website will determine whether or not there will be an in-person visit on Sunday morning.

Recently, for the first time, more books were published in digital form than in hard copy. It is basic ministry practice to have your local church newsletter online. Next, online audio, and sometimes video, and streams of sermons make your church more relevant with next generations. Email, text and social network communication between local church leaders is the norm. Utilizing online conference calls allow church leaders to have conversations without having to travel back to the city center from their homes twenty miles away. Incentives-for-decline-people will say things like "I don't have email," and complain about the terrible state of communication within the church. A conference call is out of the question for one local church leader. "If people don't have the decency to meet face-to-face then I will not participate." He resents the fact that others have difficulty attending local church meetings on campus. He lives less than one block from the church parking lot.

Telephone trees used to be the best communication tool for local churches. A telephone tree is a technique where I call you and two others, each of you call three more, and so on. It took less than two hours to get the word out. Those days are gone. Local churches use an email blast to the entire membership or post a notice on their Facebook wall. It takes minutes to communicate what used to take hours. Snail mail has declined in use. The U.S. Postal Service deficit is so bad that substations are closing, and there is a strong recommendation to eliminate Saturday delivery. Yet some "die-hards" still cling to snail mail and landline telephones as their primary tools of communication.

Parking lot conversations after worship and weekday/night meetings were formerly essential for effective communication. Now, people rush home and put their thoughts and reflections down in email or on Facebook. Is there a sense of greater transparency as this communication revolution hits the local church? We don't know, but we do believe that the ways we communicate have changed forever. We can't go back, even though some cling tenaciously to the past and have refused to join the wireless world.

Communicating in more forms and with new technology won't necessarily make the perennial council secretary and the front-lawn networkers feel better. But you will be surprised at how many older people understand the need for this technological transition. Consider this action plan:

Survey the congregation. It is surprising how many older folks know how to turn a computer on and get email from children and grandchildren.

Create and maintain an up-to-date email address for the congregation.

Establish a Facebook page and Twitter feed for the local church and invite the community to join and follow.

Offer basic email and Internet computer classes for nonusers.

Pass out hard-copy communication at every gathering of older adults.

Have a limited number of hard copies of the newsletter, past bulletins, the budget report, and the governing board minutes available in the sanctuary narthex each Sunday.

Emphasize that going wireless saves money.

PART II

The Need
for Intimacy

Today's church aims for big and splashy. Christmas pageants feature real camels and flying angels crossing the sanctuary on suspended wires. Palm Sundays have live donkeys and choirs of one hundred voices. Churches establish multiple campuses across a metropolitan area or across the country. Ironically, singles groups are so big it is difficult to meet someone. Supplies for children include the newest gadgets. Leaders have their own talk programs. In our current religious mix, it may seem impossible that anyone actually likes "smaller" better than "bigger." The majority of church members are now affiliated with large and very large churches. How can there be a payoff for being less than what you used to be?

Big and splashy, however, are also linked with some attributes that aren't so rewarding. Anonymity, depersonalization, and a certain superficiality can come with trying to make one pattern fit the masses. At least, that is the fear of persons who look to the church to fulfill their need for intimacy.

CHAPTER FOUR

The Temptation to Maintain the Status Quo

When we went to our first urban church in need of revitalization, we took a look at some recent worship bulletins. Just out of curiosity, we had the support staff pull a couple of Sunday bulletins from twenty, thirty, and forty years before. To our astonishment, the forty-year-old bulletins were no different than the current bulletins. While worship trends in the larger church had undergone radical change since the 1950s and 1960s, worship in that local church had remained unchanged for the last forty years. This isn't uncommon for churches that have been in precipitous decline for decades; it serves persons well who need to be affirmed that the way they've always done it is the right way.

There are different opinions about whether new pastors should come in and make simple changes right away or wait a year or so. Those favoring delay say showing love for the people first makes it easier to make gentle, modest changes later. The problem is what can seem like a minor change to the pastor can be major to some congregants. When we first arrived, we did little to the forty-year-old worship order. We did, however, move the pulpit about three feet from the center of the chancel. The purpose was to enable us to actually stand behind the communion table during the sacramental liturgy. Although we saw this as a minor shift on a fifty-foot chancel, all hell broke loose. One would have thought the rich history and legacy of that congregation's great preachers of the past had been trampled upon and stained beyond recognition. Those who worshiped at the feet of order, routine, and sameness were deeply disturbed.

CONFRONT WORSHIP ROUTINES

Various elements of the worship service demonstrate the need for maintenance of the status quo. Consider these three regular items:

Announcements

Not only was it important in our first revitalization assignment for the bulletin and the chancel furniture to stay the same, the announcement time needed to stay the same as well. Because the service was televised on a local cable access channel, we were able to see tapes of old worship services. Announcements averaged twelve minutes in length. Everyone knows the kind of announcements we're talking about here:

"The youth group will meet at its regular time and place tonight."

"The Esther Circle will be continuing their book study 'Making Friends' on Tuesday at 10 a.m. Please read chapter six in preparation for the time together."

"Our church administrator has this friendly reminder for us: Please, when exiting Sunday School classrooms and meeting rooms, turn out the lights! Summer is here and our energy costs have gone through the roof."

"Don't forget to give your offering to Hope for a Hungry World, and the newsletter deadline is Monday."

There were ten to twelve minutes of this every Sunday, midway through the worship service. It would not work to have announcements before the worship service because everyone was not inside the sanctuary to hear them. It would not work to have the announcements at the conclusion of worship services because people may have had to leave early and miss some important communication. It would not work to have the announcements on the sanctuary's retractable screens because there were no retractable screens in the sanctuary. Screens would deface such a sacred, holy space. People who are incentivized for decline not only like order and routine but also generally prefer order and routine that was established decades earlier. It is familiar to them, and in a rapidly changing world, familiarity is good.

While most churches identify communication as a challenge, it is less challenging to communicate in a declining church, simply because it is easier to get the word out in a small church. The smaller the church, the easier it is to know everything that is happening, and this familiarity feels comfortable to long-time members.

If I am a person who values order and a familiar routine, I might say that the purpose of the church is to make new disciples of Jesus Christ, but I will act as if the purpose of the church is to take care of my needs. If I am told that housekeeping-type announcements are off-putting or boring to visitors, I will disagree, saying that mid-service announcements are the only way I can know "what is going on." Making new disciples is secondary to the desire to be fed, to be kept comfortable, and to be kept "in the know." If Hazel comes to the microphone with the same announcement each Sunday and goes on too long, it is okay because "we know Hazel and everyone just expects that from her." Familiarity and personal fulfillment become expected.

Music

Decades ago, Ralph joined the church and immediately joined the choir. There were forty people singing regularly at the eleven o'clock service when Ralph joined. Within ten years, the choir and worship attendance both declined in numbers. The choir declined to thirty, then twenty, and now only fifteen on a good Sunday. Some were discouraged, but not Ralph.

"How's it going at church, Ralph?" a neighbor inquired.

"Pretty tough," he said. "We're not as strong as we used to be."

"What do you think is going on?" the neighbor sincerely asked.

"Oh the usual," Ralph said. "We're getting older. Young people don't seem to be as spiritual today. People aren't committed in the way they used to be, the economy, folks moving to the suburbs, that sort of thing."

"I'm sorry to hear that," the neighbor said.

"Yeah, it is tough. Our new choir director is only part-time and plays the organ as well as directing the choir. I hang in there for support. We have become a tight group over the years." But misery turns to pleasure as Ralph announces with seeming humility, "I'm singing a duet with one of our sopranos during the special music this coming Sunday! We're really scraping the bottom of the barrel now."

No matter what he says to his neighbor, it is clear that Ralph is feeling good and affirmed by his choir for what may be the first time. If Ralph could recruit a dozen new singers for his choir, his role and importance in the group might diminish. He has little or no incentive to make new disciples who might sing for Jesus Christ. The decline of his local church's music program carries with it an elevation of his status in the choir. There are persons with marginal voices who are loyal members of all local church choirs. As the choir shrinks, there are fewer soloists upon which to call. The best voices depart to sing more complex music with bigger groups. At some point, if Ralph remains loyal and regular in choir attendance, the choir will get down to a size where he is indispensible to the group. He may be asked to sing in a men's quartet, or a duet, or even a solo! For the local church the loss in quality and variety are offset by the familiarity of repeating simple choir pieces. For Ralph, as he struggles with all the other areas in life where he feels unappreciated (as we all do), this is a remarkable opportunity to shine!

Prayers

In large and growing churches, associate pastors and worship leaders pray in worship. As a church declines, though, solo pastors and shrinking numbers open the door for more lay input. Some churches have cards filled out and collected during the worship service. Then the names are read aloud from the cards and added to the prayer list for that week. In every case we've seen, having their prayer read aloud becomes more important than adding the name to prayer lists. The next step, and it's a short one, is allowing the person requesting the prayer to say it aloud over a microphone. Once microphone time takes hold, it is difficult to change.

One church experiencing this transition had a pastor who wanted to reintroduce the prayer card approach. The church had experienced a decade of decline and shrunk to seventy-five attendees on average in worship. This change in worship advocated by the pastor created enmity between the pastor and a layperson who longed for his own personal time before the people each Sunday.

Emboldened by the encouragement of one or two others, the dis-enchanted layman pounced on the new pastor:

"Do you think prayer is important?" he asked.

"Yes I do," she answered.

"Do you think we should lift up prayer concerns during worship?"

"Sure, that's appropriate in any worship service," she replied with a smile.

"There are a lot of people who think that the best way to lift up prayer concerns is to hear directly from the heart of the one pre-senting the prayer concern. It is more meaningful if done that way." And then the final push: "Many people would love to have that personal touch return to our worship services. We were hop-ing you would join us in our deep appreciation for prayers of the people."

You guessed it. The very next Sunday, prayer concerns came directly from the pews, and congregants spoke for extended peri-ods each week from that time forward. The return to the old way worked, decline continued, and the disenchanted layman had a prayer request every Sunday. Did he consciously know that growth would change worship? Possibly, but even if new people came, they rarely returned. At least they could keep worship meaningful for those still in attendance. His temptation grew stronger. The smaller the worshiping congregation, the greater the chance he had to do what he loved most: not the cause of Christ for making new disciples, but keeping the familiarity of "his" worship experience.

Many people in our society are lonely. They don't have others to talk with on a regular basis. If they have difficulty hearing, it is even harder to engage in conversation. A lot of folks just seem to need some airtime!

Someone at the microphone mentions impending surgery for herself or a family member. Another speaks up and asks for prayers for a co-worker who is hospitalized. Then someone raises a concern for a friend in another state who is ill, but feels the need to explain, over three to four minutes, how she met this friend and how long they have known each other. The next prayer concern about supporting our troops overseas comes with a complementary political agenda about how God is on the side of the United States in this conflict. A child solicits prayers for her pet. There are requests for traveling mercies, and on and on it goes.

Everyone likes the spotlight. Churches become used to this very quickly. It becomes familiar. Most people, pastors and laity alike, are simply unaware of how long they talk. Passing the microphone down the pew for prayer concerns was finally dropped by one church when the gathered worshiping congregation reached one hundred in number. The reason: too much time taken by a few.

Worship isn't the place where intimacy is developed inside a local church community. Small groups—not worship services—develop, sustain, build, and encourage intimacy.

As we have previously described, if congregants are insistent on using worship for intimacy, that worship service will never grow to more than fifty to seventy people. Intimate worship is the worship of one small group. To grow one's worship service while at the same time addressing the critical need for intimacy, one needs to start small groups outside of worship. Declining churches seem to resist this, which keeps them small.

In other words, long-established worship practices like announcements, prayer requests, and music may feel disrupted when new people come to worship. In fact, there are a couple of ways worship will change with new people participating:

1. The church that worships an average of seventy or less on Sunday morning can be intimate and have prayer concerns spoken

from the pews. The church that worships two hundred or more on Sunday morning cannot have the same feeling of intimacy in the worship experience because it is impossible for everyone to know everyone else.

2. The church that worships an average of seventy or less on Sunday morning can have mediocre-quality music if sung or played by a well-known church member whom everyone adores. In the church that worships two hundred or more on Sunday morning, where no one can know everyone in worship, higher-quality music is essential. Here is a lay member's email to us while he was on vacation. It reveals both his respect for the most intimate relationships in worship as well as his preference for the highest quality in worship music:

> I take the backcountry roads over to my sister's and have passed a rural United Methodist church for years. Sunday I stopped in for the eleven a.m. service. Attendance was twenty-one, and according to the "ladies," the membership is sixty-nine. Average age is seventy or older.

> I was early, so I sat down to enjoy the music. A woman was playing some patriotic tunes in celebration of the Fourth of July. A gentleman sat next to her at the piano and pulled out his harmonica to play along. At first I thought, "How great is this?" He was tapping his foot and belting it out. But the more I listened, the more I realized he was not very good. In fact, he was quite bad. I was thinking, "Hey, come on, buddy; maybe just play every other song. Give the gal a break."

> After about five or six numbers he turned to her and said, "Are we done?" She nodded, and he rose unsteadily. A man on the altar (the liturgist) helped him back to his seat. The old man didn't really know where he was. He was led to a pew and sat next to two older women.

I realized that the congregation was loving on a long-term member. They knew his condition, and it didn't bother them a bit that he was on the altar playing that harmonica. It was a great moment for me.

Now the kicker—during the greeting I made my way over to him and said good morning. I turned to the woman next to him and told her he played a nice harmonica. She said, "I have been married to him for sixty years. I didn't know he could play." It was beautiful. He continued to play the harmonica from his seat during the service. And it sounded pretty good to me!

New people carry their own memories of worship, sometimes classic and sometimes contemporary, into their new local churches. People like what is familiar to them. There is always a push for a "new familiar" from new people as they become more integrated into a local church. This new familiar is a threat to "keeping things the way we like them" in worship.

The goal of long-term pew sitters, who are vulnerable to temptations that cause decline, isn't to run new people off. The goal is to keep worship the way it has always been. If new people are willing to accept everything they find in this "new-to-them" local church, then they are welcome. If they like the way we worship, then come on in! If the new person comes in and, while there, begins to tinker with the way we have always done worship, then perhaps they need to find a different location in which to worship. It is the old, "If you walk, talk, look, and believe like us, welcome! If you like the things we like and like them done the way we like them done, welcome! Otherwise, there is no room in the inn."

Please understand; there are churches that worship in classic forms that are open to constantly pushing the boundaries to produce the highest possible quality of classic worship. These churches aren't imprisoned by a temptation for decline. Conversely, there are also churches that practice contemporary worship that are imprisoned by decline. It is not a matter of musical preference or worship style. These worshiping congregations aren't willing to receive and honor the diversity of outside new voices in how they express connections to God through worship. Stereotypes aren't helpful. All classic worship lovers aren't rigid and insistent on maintaining things past and all contemporary worship lovers aren't open to new and fresh, high-quality worship ideas. It is a question of how rigid the expression of worship is rather than a question of what worship form is the preference for a particular local church.

MEET THE NEED FOR FAMILIARITY IN OTHER WAYS

When eliminating announcements within the worship service, use a rolling projected image of announcements before and after the worship service itself. If you don't have projected images, use other forms of communication to spread the word about events.

Have worship assistants (ushers or acolytes) collect prayer cards during the service. Read out all the names listed on the prayer concern cards at one time.

For those who love to have visibility as worship leaders, have them do the call to the offering, telling the story of how they grew to be tithers or percentage-givers. Have the presenters write out what they will say beforehand and go over it with them.

Another option for worship is to have someone witness to his or her faith. Tell the congregation how God is active in his or her life and why she or he loves this church. Restrict to two to three minutes, written beforehand and reviewed with the primary worship leader before Sunday's worship time.

Keep quality in music with even small choirs by arranging the most gifted vocalists in quartets, trios, or even duets. Have those who aren't as musically gifted join in the chorus (along with the congregation).

CHANGE YOUR WORSHIP SPACE

Long-time members of a declining church can recall the heyday when the sanctuary was packed. They long for that feeling of excitement when activity was high and worship was an event. Before its decline, one local church averaged two hundred fifty persons in a sanctuary with a maximum seating capacity of three hundred. Attendance has steadily declined over the past two decades to an average of eighty-two per Sunday. It is now uncomfortably empty. This is the time to get the people close together again in worship, and it requires a bold plan.

If the church has pews, take out the back rows of pews across the sanctuary to recreate a sense of fullness. If the church worships in chairs, remove a percentage of chairs in the rear of the room. Target using between sixty to seventy-five percent of your sanctuary's seating capacity. Develop an incremental plan to put the pews or chairs back as the congregation achieves milestones in growth. This plan will have celebrations noted on the path forward to a full church again. Each year celebrate the percentage of growth in attendance by bringing some pews or chairs back into the worship area. Build a specific worship service around the celebration. Instill an understanding that increasing worship attendance is a part of God's plan for the kingdom. Lobby members with incentives for decline by sharing that your local church is reaching back to the glory days and will recover the close-knit feel of those times through the new plan.

What is the immediate benefit of bringing people physically closer together during worship? It helps in meeting and greeting new people in worship. It helps ushers in passing the plate. It also helps with congregational singing. If you spread eighty-two people out in a sanctuary that seats three hundred, it is difficult to hear your neighbor when singing worship music. Some pews will have just two or three people sitting in them; some may have just one individual. An empty pew may separate them. Church sociologists will say that when a congregation is at 80 percent seating capacity, it will feel completely full to a first-time visitor. The message then becomes "there is no room for me here," and we don't want that. Conversely, if the worship area has less than 50 percent of the seats occupied, the atmosphere can be depressing. The first-time visitor to a sparsely attended worship service notices the large number of empty seats and asks, "Is this church dying? What is wrong?" The ability to regulate seating to stay between 60 to 75 percent each Sunday is a huge advantage. This is the most comfortable level for church growth.

CHANGE YOUR WORSHIP SERVICE

Have special Sundays in worship such as "gospel music Sunday," "global music Sunday," or unique worship themes built into a series, and themes that follow the secular calendar (Fourth of July, Labor Day, Thanksgiving, and so on). Use the traditional pieces of liturgy, but vary them. Use all the standard creeds, have the youth write a creed, and occasionally feature a creed written by an older member of the church. Form a creative group of members to write the liturgy, and make sure their names are in the bulletin. As you grow, keep a service time that roughly follows the traditional pattern, and start another service with more innovation. If you don't have screens, begin by getting people involved in creating visuals for worship.

If people are adamant in their opposition to having projected image in worship, then try what one church did to break that opposition. Members of this local church were proud of their historic, high church, traditional worship. When some in the congregation proposed adding a retractable screen for projected image in worship, those who had benefitted from keeping worship the same mounted a protest. The proponents of the screen suggested that multisensory worship was more appealing to young adults (and they liked it too!). These were modern times and the actuary tables revealed a sobering reality of a dying church and something needed to be done now to reverse the decline. The naysayers would not be moved and launched a vigorous challenge.

It was a tradition in this local church to have a layperson give witness to his or her faith and read the morning scripture for every Sunday worship service. A pastor chose to preach a sermon series on the seven deadly sins. The pastor then went out to shut-in members of the congregation. Armed with his video camera, the pastor interviewed five persons who were unable to attend Sunday morning worship services any longer. Each person answered questions about his or her faith and love for the church before reading the scripture for the day.

One wonderful eighty-seven-year-old woman asked, "What scripture do you want me to read?"

"I want you to read the scripture lesson on lust," the pastor replied with a smile.

"Oh dear, if you are looking for recent memories, I'm afraid I won't be very helpful," she said playfully.

It was all captured on video. During the next sermon series, instead of having someone in the flesh stand and read the scripture at the appointed time, there was one of the church's long-time saints, reading the scripture to the congregation through the magic of video projection and a temporary screen. The moment brought smiles—even from those who detested any change in worship. A lay member who could no longer attend was a worship leader for a day. It was an affirmation for them and for all of the church's elderly members. It also built a strong case for one acceptable way that projected image could be used in worship.

Have "coming attractions" listed for worship during the summer. Make a brochure for the summer of all the special Sundays from June through August. Children's choir singing, barber shop quartets, ice cream socials between services, wrestling with the book of Revelation, and lots of other attractions for the summer months will keep interest up and generate excitement. Don't cancel things just because it's summer; this is a sure message of decline. Create expectancy with one or more small surprises during service each Sunday.

Teach the theological basis for every new worship activity. If you are doing baptism in a new style, explain why. If you carry the baby into the congregation, explain how the congregation is making significant promises of guidance for the life of this young child. Introduce the baby to congregational members. Explain what it means to be engrafted into the Christian faith through a particular congregation. Take the baby back to the waiting parents, and as you put that baby in their arms, remind them that this baby does not belong to them but to God, and what that means. New liturgy is much easier to introduce when it: (a) involves existing members, (b) is explained along the way, and (c) is varied and gradual.

Worship attendance is usually the last church activity we give up as we age, and its purpose is to touch and form us deep in our souls. Therefore, how worship is conducted often becomes a hot potato that cannot be touched. Especially as we grow older and contemplate meeting our maker, the sameness of worship can be comforting. Yet most declining churches don't have passionate worship, no matter how much it is enjoyed by those in the pews.

Worship can become rote, a weekly practice of going through the motions. Long-time members know many of the rubrics by heart. They love not having to look at a hymnal to say the Apostles' Creed. Yet it can make newcomers who don't know the old memorized versions feel like strangers in a strange land.

CHAPTER FIVE

The Temptation to Become an Insider

I t has happened in every local church at one time or another. A covered-dish luncheon followed the eleven a.m. worship service. The worshiping congregation moved the short distance from the sanctuary into the fellowship hall. People found their friends and joined the serving line, cafeteria style. Most were talking, some were laughing. All seemed to be having a good time settling into long-standing connections. With plates full, people moved to find a plastic molded chair and sit at one of the folding tables.

Chairs began to fill up in a way that was more reminiscent of a junior high lunchroom than a downtown church in a large metropolitan area. The pastor spied a new couple seated alone. They took a bite of their food and chewed slowly while looking around the room. They looked for connections that were either delayed in arrival or just not coming. The sight was painful. The pastor went up to the chairperson of the church's ruling body, who was still in line, and asked her to break bread with the new couple who were sitting alone. The chairperson promised to go by and meet the new couple. Then the pastor stopped at their table to chat for a few minutes. Knowing at least two good connections would be made, the pastor continued to circulate throughout the room.

Ten minutes later, the pastor looked up again and saw the new couple still alone. In another minute, the couple was gone, no one besides the pastor having shared a meal or conversation with them. Inexplicably, the chairperson was eating with long-time church friends. At the dessert table, the pastor and chairwoman met up.

"What happened?" the pastor asked.

"I don't know what you mean," answered the chairwoman.

"I thought you were going to the sit with the new couple—to eat with them and talk with them."

"I did go by and say, 'Hi, glad you came,' but I couldn't stay and eat with them."

"Why not?" the pastor asked, more confused than ever.

"I had not seen the Conroys for a couple of weeks. They are my travel partners, and this was the only time we had to discuss the overseas trip we plan to take next month."

Did they miscommunicate? Or was the desire to visit with friends simply stronger than the desire to welcome the stranger?

If a church declines and becomes smaller, it is easier to attain a feeling of intimacy, and continued decline makes it easy to keep the feeling of intimacy. More people know each others' names and histories. It isn't uncommon for members of declining churches to know the name and history of someone's parents, grandparents, and children as well. This is descriptive of one who is a local church insider.

How does one know if he or she is an insider? We have listed some criteria below which helps identify an insider.

YOU KNOW YOU ARE AN INSIDER IF . . .

You know the names of a significant percentage of the people in your worshiping congregation.

Your table is the first table that fills up at all the church luncheons.

You can recite the linear history of your congregation for the past two decades.

You were around prior to the last building campaign.

You are a carrier of "institutional memory."

You have received direct benefits of long-term membership.

"My parents and my mother's parents were members of this church for years. That should mean something," said a woman who assumed an insider role for herself. "What do you mean you won't baptize my grandbaby?"

"I didn't say I would not baptize your grandchild," said the pastor, who was working to stay pastoral while at the same time trying to communicate the length and breadth of the sacrament's meaning. "I just said that I would like to talk to your daughter and her husband first about what baptism means. I would like them to come to church and give evidence that they intend to raise the child in this church as their home congregation."

Entitlement and intimacy can become intertwined for some church members. These are insider claims. At the 2010 session of the Desert Southwest Annual Conference, Clif Christopher said church membership doesn't necessarily have its privileges, church membership has its responsibilities. Church members may be tempted to use longevity as a means of entitlement. There is a direct correlation between strong feelings of entitlement and ongoing decline. There is payoff in smaller, more intimate communities. It is easier for any community of faith to better understand its lofty status and earned prestige if the community grows smaller. Strangers and new persons are without knowledge of long-term members' roles and history in the church.

Oftentimes, the insider, filled with entitlement and wanting his or her congregation to feel intimate, will insist that the church remain just as it has always been. These congregants generally have a high need for stability and security in their lives. If change is coming fast and furious in other areas of life, then they cling to the stability and security of an unchanging church. For people whose highest values are stability, security, and comfort for everyone, there is no more favorite refusal to change than, "We have never done it that way before."

If it is true that "the local church has never done it that way before," it is likely that the speaker will finish the pronouncement with, "and we aren't going to start doing it that way now."

This becomes a good litmus test for self-assessment. If we are members who recoil at the possibility of trying on some new programmatic idea or entering into a new process for connecting people to Jesus Christ, then we may be flirting with "insider temptation." When we are stuck on entitlement, with an insider mentality, a "me first" attitude will likely emerge.

Consider how church consultant Reggie McNeal distinguishes the "internal" (me first) church and the "external" (transform the world) church. The internally focused church has different questions from the externally focused church:

INTERNAL	EXTERNAL
(persons with incentive to decline)	(persons who embrace growth)
* Where is my blessing?	* Where have I been a blessing to others?
* What activities meet my needs?	* What activities reach out to others?
* What do I want in worship?	* What worship activities will attract others?
* How does my church serve me?	* How does my church serve others?

Clearly both internal and external elements of church life are important. The problem emerges with persons who believe the internal focus takes priority over the external focus. We must educate church people that the external focus is the true purpose of the local church. The pathway of revitalization is moving from internal questions to external questions. For those who cling to the "me first" personal benefits of decline, this path will be very hard to walk.

A prominent couple in one church we served made an appointment to see us. After moments of polite conversation, the husband, holding his wife's hand, frowned and spoke his mind.

"We thought long and hard about coming to talk with you. We aren't persons who complain, but there is something that is impossible for us to ignore any longer. As our pastors, we thought you both should know. Lily and I aren't being fed by our church."

Over the course of ministry, often clergy develop a tendency in their work to try to keep everyone happy. As young clergy, we attended a continuing education event where the leader suggested that out of all the vocations, clergy had the highest need to be liked. In fact, both judicatories and congregations support this behavior. Clergy are rewarded for behavior that says things like, "I am so sorry, how can I help you feel more connected? Just tell me what it is I have done to cause your dissatisfaction, and I will do my best to correct my mistakes. We want you to be happy here." (This may be exaggerated, but you get the drift.)

Afraid that long-standing pillars of the church might withhold money, stop coming to worship, or sow discord among the congregation during the "meeting after the meeting" in the parking lot, we wondered if there was another way to look at the situation, an approach that went beyond "fixing" the problem.

In an approach more direct than gentle, John asked, "Who are you feeding?"

"Excuse me?" the husband responded, unsettled and taken aback.

"Who are you feeding?" John repeated.

"We find that there is a connection between our engagement in active ministry to others, and the feeling of being spiritually inspired or fed," Karen explained.

As you might expect, the couple sitting before us was not happy with this turn in the conversation. In truth, their pattern of church participation had been limited to regular worship and committee meeting attendance. There was no active, hands-on ministry with others, the key ingredient to building an externally driven church. Eventually this couple led a "walkout" of the church one Sunday morning, carrying with them their picture of Jesus, which they had presented to their Sunday school class as a gift. They joined a nearby church, which remained a bastion against the demographics of their changing neighborhood.

CHAPTER SIX

The Temptation to Limit Church Size

W hat do pews, columbaria, sidewalk bricks, and local church histories have in common? In many churches, these are the places where people can find names of families who are forever linked with their local churches. On the support rails of many church pews, little brass nameplates note the "giver" of that pew. Some historic churches have a columbarium, where for enough money, a member's ashes can be placed and their names prominently displayed on a wall until Jesus comes.

At some churches there are commemorative bricks on sidewalks with names inscribed, noting a contribution that was made toward construction or enhancement of a space to give a feeling of serenity and repose. Additionally, church histories venerate long-time church families and name charter members and significant church leaders through the years.

These are all local church attempts to satisfy our insatiable thirst to know and be known. In life and in death, we want to be remembered. If a local church is growing, there is pressure to learn new names. This pressure makes us uncomfortable. We all know learning new names means we care. However, if the local church is in decline, it is easier to care for people because there are fewer people to care about. If a church is growing, we look for our friends on a Sunday morning and miss them in a sea of new faces. However, if a church is in decline, we can easily spot a friend sitting in the pew where she always sits, and everything seems okay, even though there are fewer of us. We will catch a friend, speak a personal word, and then repeat the process with nearly everyone we care about on a Sunday morning.

The simple fact is that it is easier to know someone's name when there are fewer names to know. In addition, when names are on display in one or more of the ways that local churches display their members' names, we are reminded of the members' lives and of their perceived importance when we pass by that location. As a local church declines, budgets become tighter and the local church must find ways to take assets and turn them into revenue producers.

There are many pros and cons to the church's common practice of commemorative gifts. Among the cons:

It can easily get out of hand, with plaques on everything from hymnals to furniture.

The naming practice can lead to a rigid insistence that the items given in the church can't be changed because it will hurt the giver.

It can make new people feel they are visiting a museum instead of a vibrant worshipping community.

Recognition is often tied to how much you can afford to give, a practice antithetical to the gospel.

SATISFY THE NEED TO BE KNOWN AND CARED FOR

Commemorative gifts also serve the vital purpose of creating intimacy. The practice of naming can be life-giving both to the local church's budget as well as to families who want to feel their loved ones won't be forgotten. One church established a memorial in a large alcove off a major hallway. (Any entry hall would work just as well.) All the plaques were removed from their locations on furniture and walls and gathered together in the one area. Long-time church members could visit the area anytime, and the area was large enough for the gifts of future generations.

Once the plaque area is established, it stays up no matter what happens to the gift, freeing the church to make changes as needed. Whenever a memorial gift is no longer used, such as furniture, art-work, and so on, it may be offered back to the donating family with the words: "Now that we're redecorating the parlor, we wanted you to have this painting your mother gave as our gift to you. It has meant so much to us over the years, and of course, the plaque is still in the Memorial Room."

Intimacy is critical to any local church and extends beyond the use of gifts and memorial plaques. Persons captured by incentives to decline often insist on intimacy in worship. These folks may be educated that the purpose of worship is many things:

Praising God and Christ.

Growing connectedness with God and Christ.

Hearing the word of God read and proclaimed.

Experiencing the energy and power of communal worship.

Transforming the human heart and mind.

Encouraging Christians to go out into the world and serve.

Intimacy with God.

The purpose of worship isn't to provide the kind of personal attention and affirmation that is available through small groups. John Wesley understood the need for small group formation and participation for believers to become disciples. Declining churches treat worship as a small group process, and small groups can only function for intimacy when they are small! How many? The number probably varies, but twelve to fifteen seems to work in most contexts. If your congregation has fifty people in worship and is trying to let worship meet the needs of intimacy and caring, worship size will inevitably be reduced to a manageable number. People need intimacy and need to feel cared for. Satisfy this need for intimacy through small groups, rather than worship.

PURSUE SMALLNESS AGGRESSIVELY

Small groups need to begin with conversation. Look over the members and friends of your local church and find what things people have in common. Make a list of common touchpoints then issue an invitation for conversation. Don't simply put an announcement in the worship bulletin but make personal, one-on-one, face-to-face invitations. Complete a discerning process with persons you hope will participate in the small group as design team members. Ask questions like "What dates are best?" and "What time during the day or night works best?" If the target group has small children in the home: "Do we need childcare?" or "What location will be best for getting the maximum number of people to attend?"

Of course, the need for small groups isn't new information. But consider aggressive pursuit in getting people into the conversation. Note, we are changing the language from "issue invitations" to "aggressive pursuit" of persons you would like to see participate. We practice aggressive pursuit. Aggressive pursuit looks like this:

"Bob, many folks in our area have lost their jobs just like you. I know it has been tough for you, and I am impressed with your spirit and resolve through this difficult time. Yours is a powerful story and model for people going through this. We are having a gathering of people who have all lost their jobs in this awful economy. We need you to be at that gathering. Yours is a compelling story, and your attitude has continued to be positive. Your spirit is infectious. We have to have you at the gathering. Say you will come!"

"Judy, I see you are a stay-at-home mom with teenagers. I know you juggle ten things at once, and you always seem to keep it together in situations that overwhelm others."

Judy replies, "Oh, I'm not so sure about that," pleased with the affirmation.

"But you are good at what you do. . . . We are having all the friends and members of our church to our house on Tuesday night to talk about the joys and frustrations of parenting teenagers. We need you there."

"Sam, we are beginning a ROMEO group—Retired Old Men Eating Out. Some guys are having trouble adjusting to retirement. They don't seem to know what to do with themselves, and their wives are ready to kick them out of the house. You have said that the first few months of retirement were tough for you, but now, two years later, you've got a lot of things going, and you appear to be really happy to be retired."

Sam agrees, "You're right. At first it was difficult to deal with finding a purpose, something meaningful, but I think I came through it all right."

"Here is the deal. . . . We need you to come to this first lunch group meeting on Wednesday noon at Mary's restaurant. We are inviting all the recently retired guys from the church, friends and members alike. Maybe you know some guys who fit our description but don't come to church. If so, bring them along. It is important for the church and other retired guys for you to be there."

Here is a list of needs within a congregation that call for formation of small groups:

Loss of a job

Stay-at-home moms

Retirees

Surrogate grandparents

Avid readers for "book of the month"

Young adults (for whatever constitutes "young" in your congregation)

People in recovery

Movie lovers

Play dates for preschoolers and parents

Blended families

Covenant groups for spiritual growth

Whatever is of interest and will bring people together in an introductory conversation may become a potential small group. Inside of this and subsequent conversations, relationships will be established, and relationships will deepen over time. People will begin to socialize together within the membership of a particular small group. They will begin to sit together in worship. Leaders will emerge, and as the congregation experiences new growth, they will guide the group in congregational care of the small group's members. Research by Towers and Watson shows that churches with 350 persons or more in worship need at least thirty-eight small groups for the church to be vital and their members to feel connected. Churches with 100 to 349 in worship need at least twelve groups; churches with less than one hundred in worship need three to five small groups.

Recruit small group leaders with the understanding that they will be the "care leaders" for that small group. It is most easily seen in long-term adult Sunday school classes, but the best class leaders practice caregiving leadership when members of small groups have medical or personal crises. If the structure is correctly built, the one in need of caregiving will first call his or her small group leader even before they would call the pastor. (As a pastor you don't just need to be okay with that; you need to be happy about it!)

There are many excellent resources for building small groups. Google "starting small group ministries" and begin to explore. Members who insist that worship be the place for intimacy need not hold churches captive. Instead, reactivating small group ministry is the pathway to close relationships for more people and increased vitality for the local church.

For each small group meeting in the local church—administrative, social, or programmatic—try starting with a "check in" or a "get acquainted" exercise for people to become accustomed to a small group process. Here is how we do a "check-in":

"As our first order of business, let's do a check-in. We go around the room and everyone says their name and how they are feeling right now. Everyone answers the question of what is going on in his or her life. Please limit yourselves to three or four sentences—no more. I'll go first, to model this for those who are new to the group. 'My name is John. I am feeling anxious about our time together. I am hoping I have properly prepared for our time together. My son's birthday is today, and I look forward to returning home to help the family celebrate.'"

"OK, I'm Kathie, and I feel tired after a long day at work."

"I'm Terry. This is my first time. If I appear distracted, it is because I just got a call that my mother has been admitted to the hospital and they are running tests."

"I'm Frank, and my world is great!"

We continue around the table until everyone has had a chance to speak. When we return to John, rather than diving into the stated agenda he departs with this:

"I'm still thinking about Terry and her mom," he begins. "I wonder if we could hear a little more from her, and then pray together for her mom?"

No one spoke more than four sentences. No one dominated, and they all shared something personal about themselves. Everyone was included. Some came with no stress whereas others were highly stressed. Terry was new. She was asked to share her real feelings in the moment. She accepted the risk and spoke her anxiety out loud. Everyone around the table got to know her better as she talked about her mother's health concerns. She felt accepted and included. It was real and relational. The group prioritized her concern and prayed an intercessory prayer for her mother.

Check-in helps us get to know one another. Check-in helps us understand one another. Without a check-in, the group might have rocked along in this gathering without any understanding about why Terry appeared distracted and not fully present. She is new, so few people know her. They might question what positive things she can bring to the group if she is there for the entire hour but never says a word. When there is no check-in, impressions are formed and assumptions are made.

The key is to structure ways in which people can get to know each other better. In a church that is unaccustomed to having new people in groups or new people serving in church offices, the presence of new faces can be unsettling or uncomfortable. To have a specific plan for people to get to know each other better at every gathering is a key to assimilation. Even if everyone around the table is a longtime church member, it is beneficial to know how everyone is feeling in that moment. When the gathered community is practiced in this or a similar exercise, there is an advantage in every small group gathering. Even if a person is new to the small group, doing a check-in will become a familiar practice.

If the worship service dips below fifty, even four small groups can be hard to nurture and sustain. Some churches of fewer than fifteen to twenty families, with average ages over seventy-five, may not support the implementation of small group ministry. Church consultant Gil Rendle starkly states the problem facing declining churches across the country: "Some churches are not going to be able to endure that second birth, but they are able to think clearly about how their original purpose might be carried into an uncertain future."[1]

A "legacy church" is a congregation that is resigned to its decline, yet determined to pass on a legacy to a new congregation. Its lay people vote to continue the flow of ministry as it is, and the pastor agrees to provide worship leadership, visit hospitals, and conduct funerals—on a part-time basis.

The other duties are focused on growing a new congregation in the same location. The existing congregants get their wish to limit change, recognizing their pathway to extinction is inevitable. They are choosing to respond to Ezekiel's prophetic words about the dry bones: "I will cause breath to enter you, and you shall live" (Ezekiel 37:5).

71

Gil Rendle has proposed an effective model for this much-needed step, and the Southwest Texas Conference of the United Methodist Church has experimented with this in Austin. It is a radical step, only necessary when forces of decline combine, such as age, spiritual maturity, location, and finances, and the available leadership and energy for small group formation no longer exists. Perhaps an individual congregation can bequeath its heart, history, and property to a new start. Throughout our cities, there are many candidates.

PART III
The Need for
Affirmation

We've explored what it looks like when a church tries to fill the needs of its members for power and intimacy. What does it look like when a declining church tries to affirm the ministry of others? Sometimes it means we start to throw money and attention at it, like with children and youth; sometimes it means we ignore the ministry because they don't really need us, like church preschools. Other times it means we just pile more and more responsibility on "our wonderful staff."

CHAPTER SEVEN

The Temptation
to Become
Child-Focused

As youth and children's programs are often the first to
decline in numbers, those who remain receive more
resources and attention. Where one local church had a
youth group that numbered over one hundred teens on Sunday
night, it now averages between ten and twelve. Sometimes it has
as few as six teens at a Sunday night gathering. One pastor
describes this scene:

> Early on in my ministry there, I dropped in on our Sunday night
> senior high youth group meeting. Here is the upside:
>   It was an interesting Sunday night program.
>   A charismatic youth director led the program.
>   There were six adult sponsors in the room.
> This is the downside:
>   The youth director planned and implemented the entire pro-
> gram without sponsor help.

There were only six senior high kids in the room; more adults than teens attended.

We were spending about $2,000 per teenager each year in the program, according to average attendance on any given Sunday night.

In our most cynical moments, we have wondered, "Why not pay every senior higher $1,000 per year to show up on Sunday nights?" Even if we allow four absences per year, it is a win/win situation: kids get the money and we can report that we have doubled the size of our youth program. Of course, you can't buy discipleship.

Parents and teenagers who attend local churches that have experienced decades of decline receive more resources and attention as the church gets smaller. This senior high youth group meeting had a greater than 1:1 ratio of adult leaders to teens. The church sends its teens on a mission trip every year to faraway places, financed by a youth line item that has stayed the same in dollars since the days of fifty-plus in attendance. Every fourth year it is an international mission trip. When you have the same amount of dollars for twenty that used to serve fifty, even factoring in inflation, that is a bundle!

Many local church foundations have a membership reward. A scholarship for college is granted to qualifying youth. Fifteen years ago the average scholarship amount was $500 a year; with so few youth, the average annual amount now awarded is $1,000 to $1,500. If I am a teenager and I have grown up in this church, I can count on a similar scholarship amount each of my (first) four years of undergraduate education.

Several teens and parents in this particular local church don't seem interested in growing the youth group, but they are powerfully tempted to maintain the youth scholarship program. There is a huge possible reward beginning in high school and ending with an undergraduate degree. There is one small intimate group with six to twelve persons where youth can connect and, some Sundays, receive one-on-one attention from an adult who wants to be a friend.

What happens if there is an infusion of new life? What happens if the group doubles or triples to twenty or thirty each Sunday evening? Now the attention of adult sponsors will have to be shared with four to five others. There is a cap on scholarship money so now maybe the awards are $300 to $500 per year instead of $1,500, as in previous years. If half of my international mission trip was paid for through a combination of line item budget and youth fundraising projects (car washes where I didn't necessarily have to show up to get the benefits, and when I did show up, the adult counselors did most of the work), and now we have to split that thirty ways instead of six, then my church world just got more difficult. Why would I want to invite newcomers to the Sunday night group? Teens generally prefer a bigger group, yet there is an incentive to keep it small.

Children in declining church programs fare similarly. The ratios of adult leaders to children are better in Sunday school at a declining church than in a growing church. If the declining church can maintain some level of critical mass, that is, enough kids to have a fun activity but not too many to force sharing the leaders' undivided attention, or recruit twice as many teachers, then it can feel intimate and cozy. These children may benefit by receiving scholarships to children's camp as long as the local church continues in decline.

Declining churches bemoan the lack of children but are unwilling to do what it takes to attract children to the church. We post signs that say "No Skateboarding." We offer them ancient, worn-out gym equipment. We quit volunteering for VBS and teaching Sunday school because, "We already did that." We expect them to behave in church as we do, or at least as our children did, refusing to recognize that everything changes—including the best ideas for growing children into healthy adults. We neglect church nurseries. We decide we need more youth Sundays and more children's sermons. All the while, what is really needed is for the adults in the church to actually support the children and youth ministries with their prayers, their presence, their money, and their service.

In one church that has been in decline for decades, some leaders hungered for the presence of young families in their congregation. Recognizing that a well-positioned and well-equipped church nursery was vital in attracting young families, it was proposed that a room next to the sanctuary be converted to an up-to-date, modern nursery.

"We have a perfectly adequate nursery on campus," one older adult remarked.

"But it is located in another building, across the church campus, and it has cribs that are no longer produced because they have been proved to be hazardous for babies and toddlers," a new young adult leader in the church said. "That room, right next to the sanctuary, would be perfect for our nursery."

"There is a stained glass window in the room you are talking about. A long-time member family of our church contributed that window thirty years ago. They should at least be consulted before we make such a change," advised a longtime leader.

Before the next meeting of the local church governing board, someone talked to the grandson of the family that had contributed the memorial window. This surviving family member said, "A nursery would not be in keeping with what our family had in mind when we donated that window to the church." Paralyzed by the incentive for decline of one long-term member's descendent, the motion for an updated, conveniently located nursery was tabled, never to surface again.

All the while, the laments never cease: "What's happened to all our children?" "Why don't they come to church?"

MOVE FROM CHILD/YOUTH-FOCUSED TO CHILD/YOUTH-FRIENDLY

Children are the church's best hope because they are the future of the church, not because they change our demographics. Children force adults to keep a fresh face on the world. To keep up with them, we have to keep up with the changes that happen all around us. Through their eyes, issues that have stubbornly divided us can be seen differently. For example, consider the issue of inclusivity. We are created to practice community. The Christian gospel insists that all persons who love Jesus Christ are welcome in our local church. However, for some adults, this behavior is hard to model.

The number one factor declining churches could change, and thereby attract more young people, is authenticity in our practice of the gospel. Young people can sense inauthenticity, and it is one of the reasons they cite for avoiding the church: "They aren't real," or "They don't practice what they preach." We lost many people over this issue in the sixties when too many local churches refused to embrace integration. We should have been leaders in the movement; instead we paid lip service through denominational stances. Today our wars are over such issues as homosexuality, music, and styles of worship. Our young people are looking at us, thinking, *Who did you say is your Lord?*

If you still have some children left in your church, you're lucky. Take a long, hard look at what you're modeling for them. We can educate our children and youth to look for the "right kind of people" to hang out with, or we can educate them to accept everyone just as they are and welcome them into our local church family. We can educate our children to only give time to people who look, act, talk, and dress like them, or we can educate them that God created all the people of the world to live as brothers and sisters. We can drop our children off, or we can stay and enroll in courses ourselves during Sunday morning and evening. In doing so, we model the need for ongoing spiritual growth. We can allow petty disagreements about items that don't matter, or we can make sure that church conflicts are only about matters that strike at the heart of the gospel. We can gossip and complain about anyone in our church, or we can truly practice the teachings of Paul, who cautioned us against these destructive behaviors because they undermine the foundations of the church. We can teach a rigid rule of who is in and who is out, or we can teach that the local church follows the Christ who says, "You shall love the Lord your God with all your heart, and with all your soul, and with all your strength, and with all your mind; and your neighbor as yourself" (Luke 10:27).

Teach young people that "less for us means more for the world." Young people know that we need to recycle. Young people know that we produce enough food in the world to feed everyone, but we have a distribution problem. Young people know that Styrofoam will live forever in our landfills. Young people know that the world's resources are limited, and we are called to be eco-friendly and limit our carbon footprint. Young seekers of the Christian faith can be effective models for resistant adult disciples. Host eco-fairs in your church parking lot. (Numerous community organizations will be glad to set up booths. You provide the biblical context.) Make sure your church has environmental and conservation practices.

No church without a hands-on, active mission program can attract young people. It's the one thing the church has historically done that has power for young adults. Too often, our adult mission efforts are carried on by a faithful few, while the rest just write an occasional check to salve the conscience.

Shane Claiborne, author of *Irresistible Revolution* and a leader among Christian young adults, led worship with young people in Austin, Texas. Shane told of a local church in San Antonio that was reaching out to the desperately poor by opening their doors to them every Sunday morning. "What that church's clothes closet needs more than anything is shoes. Homeless people have no place to go, they walk all day long, and their feet are tired. Many come to the church looking for shoes." One by one, a trickle grew into a crowd. The young people came forward, took off the shoes on their feet and left them at the altar. Most teens and young adults went home barefoot that night.

The pastor of that San Antonio church received delivery of the shoes from Austin and placed them in front of her local church's altar the following Sunday. As she told the story of what happened with those young Christians in Austin, adults began to rise from their seats. These adults came forward, took off their shoes, added them to the pile in front of the altar, and returned to their seats. The Holy Spirit was in that sanctuary. Adults of all ages left worship in their stocking feet. That's authenticity.

We must believe this and teach our children and youth that until our local churches want the poor inside our walls so we can worship, study, and celebrate together, we risk betrayal of the gospel's heart. Most of the mission work done by local churches is "drive-by ministry." Drive-by ministry is where we go to the social problems of the world but never bring them up close and personal inside our congregations. It isn't that drive-by ministry is bad; it's just inadequate. When we stand in the same bread line for Holy Communion, when we listen to the prayer concerns of a refugee from the Sudan, when we hear the story of a recovering addict, (not once, but week in and week out), our hearts and minds are transformed after the example of Christ. When we go downtown to work in a shelter or across the U.S. border to build a house, we manage to keep the problems of modern society a safe distance away, and that safe distance is antithetical to Christ, who threw in his lot with the least, the last, and the lost (Luke 16:19-41). Inconveniently, even kids know that.

Sharing, generosity, and welcoming of the sojourner create the climate we want for our children. What impact will this climate have when scholarship time rolls around? Earlier we spoke of taking a "me first" spirit to the scholarship committee of the local church. A scholarship committee meeting looks different when the question for these decision makers is "Who really needs scholarship assistance?" rather than treating this as an entitlement of members. Even better, if you live in a town with any kind of higher education, change your scholarship program to bring young people into your church, instead of sending them off to college with a little pocket change. Offer scholarships to local college students to work with youth, teach Sunday school, work in the church office, direct a children's choir, work in the nursery, drive a van to pick up others, and so on. Not only will you be helping young people, you will be keeping them involved in church during an age when they typically drop out.

Resist collapsing the ages of your Sunday school into one big class. Resist even for the summer. If you can't staff the Sunday school with enough volunteers, it's time for a church-wide meeting about the problem. Everyone isn't gifted to work with youth and children, but they are gifted in other ways: They can prepare meals, drive vans to pick up children who can't come otherwise, tutor, lead hikes, take attendance on Sunday mornings, and renovate rooms. The possibilities overflow. Children's and youth ministry cannot belong to a staff member. It has to belong to the whole congregation or it will die. We must stop hiring people to charm our children and youth and roll up our sleeves to pitch in.

THRIVING PRESCHOOLS AND DECLINING CHURCHES

Church preschools are a well-established practice across denominations, in rural settings and in cities, in affluent churches and in hard-hit neighborhoods. With more parents working, it is a needed ministry and a good use of our buildings. Without caring for children during the week, most of our churches would sit empty Monday through Friday. In too many places, though, the preschool is separated from the church, thinking of itself as more of a tenant than a part of the church's neighborhood outreach ministry. Some were even set up this way deliberately, in a misguided attempt to do mission without involving faith. In our efforts to affirm the church preschool, we have allowed it to operate increasingly independently and autonomously. It is probably this landlord- tenant relationship that has chipped away the vitality and possibilities for growth that every preschool embodies. So potent a force for growth is a church's preschool that many nondenominational churches will plant a church by first opening a preschool! The families in the preschool become the hub for a new church start.

A church in Phoenix lowered its average member age from the mid-fifties to the mid-thirties in only nine years. How? They established a deep connectedness with their preschool that had become increasingly separate from the church. It wasn't easy. For example, the preschool gave a discount to the children of persons who were church members, and these children were first on the waiting list. Naturally, many people joined to receive this perk. As a step toward increasing the connectedness, the church simply changed its policy by adding two important adjectives to the word "member." These perks would now go only to the children of participating and contributing members. They defined this as any member who was present in worship more than half the Sundays of the year (twenty-seven Sundays) and made a pledge of at least one dollar per year. Pretty minimal definition, isn't it?

Yet you can imagine the flak this caused. One family came into the pastor's office and said, "We are very disappointed, Pastor, in the church's new policy regarding the preschool. It seems very judgmental to us. Twenty-seven Sundays is a lot to expect from young families. You're just going to drive people away."

"But this is what it means to be a member of this church. It means you attend here; it means you support us with your prayers, presence, gifts, and service," said the pastor. "We aren't really changing anything. We're just defining our expectations. What do you think our vows of membership mean?"

"That isn't the point! The point is you are imposing a new legalism on people; that's just not who we are. We're more open. You're ruining this church and taking the preschool down with you."

All this came from a family whose children were not even in the preschool at the time! Gradually, the controversy subsided. Chapel was instituted, first weekly and voluntarily, but nine years later, it is held every day and simply part of the preschool's daily routine. If we cannot reach the people who drive into our parking lot every day to drop off their children, how can we hope to reach the neighborhood around us?

If the relationship between your church and your preschool is distant or combative, then it means the young families who know you best are actually a negative force for advertising your congregation. No church can afford this kind of relationship. Imagine this conversation:

"I know your children are in the First Church Preschool, and I hear it is a great program," Jim said to his friend.

"Oh, it is. All our children have gone there and loved it," Bob said enthusiastically.

"Good to know. We're looking for a church; maybe we'll try that one," said Jim.

"Oh, we don't go to church there," Bob replied, trailing off.

"Why not?" Jim asked.

Who knows how Bob will answer. Maybe he'll say he's never met the pastor or doesn't know anyone there. Maybe he'll say he just doesn't go to church. Maybe he'll say that his children are already there Monday through Friday. Maybe he'll say none of the teachers or the director attend church there either, or even that they don't like the church. One thing is for sure. It's unlikely his friend, Jim, will put your church on his list of places to visit.

Preschools are often filled with we/they and us/them language. Turf battles abound. The separation grows even stronger when our misguided attempts to communicate acceptance of all people becomes more a message of disinterest in the faith lives of young families and the spiritual formation of preschoolers.

In declining churches that still hold children's Sunday school, cauldrons of boiling resentment erupt between church and preschool over lockers, space, supplies, cleaning, and maintenance. Financial conflict is inevitable. Is the church subsidizing the preschool, or has the preschool grown so big and powerful that it is subsidizing the operating budget of the church? All this evidences the fact that the preschool, initially conceived as a ministry, has become nothing more than a tenant.

Ask yourself these questions:

Are your preschool board members also church members?

Do the board members actually attend worship and support children's ministry?

Do the preschool director and/or any of the teachers attend worship?

Does the director attend church staff meetings?

Does the church staff attend preschool "back to school" night, Christmas programs, and so on?

Does a church staff member sit on the school board?

Before your local church gives up the idea of the preschool/church relationship altogether:

Institute a weekly chapel time for the children and work toward daily chapel. Focus on making it child-friendly! Help the children have fun. There are many resources that share our Christian values without indoctrination or judging other religions.

Teach the children songs and have them sing in worship.

Make sure a group from the congregation attends the preschool's "back to school" gatherings. Do the cooking for a dinner; serve refreshments.

Have a Friday Night Out once a month for parents of preschool children. Staff the childcare with volunteers from the church. Plan fun activities and make them free or charge a very small fee (cheaper than the local area's babysitting costs). Advertise it through the preschool.

Include the preschool parents on your mailing list.

Visit the children who attend preschool when they are hospitalized or a death occurs in the family. Make sure the preschool director informs the pastor of all pastoral matters.

Have a group from the church knit baby blankets for newborns of preschool families.

Have a special Sunday in fall and spring emphasizing the preschool as part of your outreach ministry. Invite parents to attend.

Serve good coffee to the parents as they drop off their children in the morning (really good coffee—ask a young person if you're not sure what this entails in today's market).

Make sure the preschool board is made up of a majority of (active, participating) church members. Require that the director and the board chairperson be church members.

Host a graduation time for the oldest children as they transition into public schools. Make sure it is fun and meaningful as a life transition.

Don't do any programming without at least trying to think of a way to connect it with your church's preschool.

This is so important that if your preschool isn't set up this way, amend the bylaws. Many were set up this way initially, but the practice was reduced to paying lip service to these expectations. That has to change. A tenant who doesn't value what you do as a church is the worst kind of PR you can have.

CHAPTER EIGHT

The Temptation to Push Ministry on Clergy and Paid Staff

L est we believe that the temptations of church only afflict laity, consider this: If a church is growing rapidly, greeting at the door after a worship service is much more difficult for the pastor as well. Trying to remember the names of new persons is very frustrating. Finding a new person and connecting that visitor with a longtime member of similar age or life station is hard work. Making sure that the systems of retrieving data from a new family, including name, address, email, telephone, how long they have lived in the area, what they do during the day, and so on, is also hard work. With all that is expected of pastors, and with a church that doesn't seem to want to grow, it is easy to place "making new disciples" at the bottom of the pile. With pastors, an often-unrecognized temptation is that a shrinking church means less work for the same amount of pay—at least for a while. Even as our local churches shrink in size, salaries of clergy, or beloved lay staff members, rarely shrink as fast as attendance and membership.

The math is simple: same size staff plus dwindling number of persons in attendance equals more attention for individual members by the existing staff. If the staff responds by meeting the needs of the flock, deep loyalty can spring up. Beloved staff members can be kept on due to the depth of their relationships with certain powerful church members even though they are ineffective in their work.

This pastoral incentive for decline fits synergistically with the need of many parishioners for more personal, pastoral, and programmatic attention. It's hard for congregations, staff, and pastors to give that up, in spite of its inward focus. When pastors hang on to a need to be important, no lay visitation program can hope to succeed. It will be undermined by the pastor's need to be needed. For lay pastoral visitation to work, it must be fully supported by the pastor. Even then, the congregation's members may resist.

One local church had made enough progress in its growth to gather together a group of lay people for the purpose of prayer and visitation. Prayers were made for those in the congregation who were experiencing illness; hospitalization; family issues; or emotional, spiritual, or financial struggles. At the end of their one-hour-long gathering, individual members of the group received their visitation assignments to the homebound and hospitalized. The purpose of laity taking leadership in this ministry is to redirect paid staff toward leadership training for outreach and evangelization. Immediately the new program ran into a roadblock.

"Hello, Martha," the lay visitor said upon entering Martha's hospital room. "I'm part of the new congregational care team from the church."

"My church?" Martha questions.

"Our church," Jack corrects, as gently as he can. "We go to the same church, and I am on the new congregational care team."

"My church doesn't care about me anymore, so it's nice that you're here," Martha complains.

"My goodness! Why would you say something like that?" Jack asks, clearly concerned.

"Because since I came to the hospital, no one from the church has come to visit me," Martha explains.

"Martha," Jack says, working hard to understand. "I have come to visit you."

"But, I mean, no one from the church has come to visit me," Martha repeats, wondering why Jack seems confused.

"Martha," Jack patiently explains, "I am from the church, and I bring the church's concerns and prayers to your bedside. Your church is thinking of you and praying for you every day."

"Well, you're not Pastor Glen!" Martha protests. "Pastor Glen has not been here. In my day, the pastor always visited the hospitals, sometimes twice a week. Apparently Pastor Glen cares nothing about the long-term members of his church!"

"Pastor Glen will visit everyone who is hospitalized and calls to request a visit from the pastor," Jack repeats an oft-spoken communication used in many of his hospital visits.

"He should know that I am here sick. I told my friends, and I'm sure they must have told him. I shouldn't have to call the church office and ask for a visit!"

"I am here now, representing the church. May I pray with you?" Jack answers, trying to redirect Martha and feeling inadequate.

"If you want," Martha says dismissively.

Martha wants personal, pastoral attention while she is in the hospital, and to her, there is no substitute. Prayers of the people may be well and good, but she believes they can hardly carry the power with God that prayers from the pastor will carry. She does not like the direct correlation she notices between a growing church and diminishing personal pastoral attention. She would rather see her church decline and return to a pastor who makes all the hospital visits rather than share this ministry with the laity. She is affirming the importance of the pastor to her personally.

Martha needs to be reintroduced to the book of Acts, where the needs of the early church grew, and deacons were appointed to take care of the widows and the needy.

> In those days when the number of disciples was increasing, the Grecian Jews among them complained against the Hebraic Jews because their widows were being overlooked in the daily distribution of food. So the Twelve gathered all the disciples together and said, "It would not be right for us to neglect the ministry of the word of God in order to wait on tables. Brothers, choose seven men from among you who are known to be full of the Spirit and wisdom. We will turn this responsibility over to them and will give our attention to prayer and the ministry of the word." (Acts 6:1-4 NIV)

Martha is correct in her assumption that church growth is to blame for her lack of personal attention from the pastor. A growing church in the earliest days required help from the pews, and it is no different now. Martha will say that she wants to unite new faces as disciples for Jesus Christ. However, if that means she loses the visit from her ordained pastor, she will back away from embracing the evangelistic purpose of the local church because she loves receiving personal attention. It seems the temptation exists among both laity and clergy to force the work of ministry on paid clergy and staff.

When pastoral and staff leaders have learned how to empower laity for ministry, there is less one-on-one time with individual parishioners. This isn't just true in hospital visits, but in programmatic and administrative areas as well. Outrageous as it might seem to some, the pastor of Martha's church has even missed some board meetings, trustees meetings, and finance committee meetings on occasion. This pastor teaches the leaders of the local church and equips the local church leaders to pastor the members of their local church.

Truthfully, Martha prefers her declining church to the days when it had eight hundred people in worship. She values a pastor who would never dream of turning hospital visitation over to "amateurs." She likes an open-door policy where she can drop by the church office and spend thirty minutes sitting in the pastor's office, sharing pleasant conversation. Her incentive isn't to grow the church but, on the contrary, to help the church decline. In declining churches, people are more likely to receive personal attention, not just from pastoral staff, but from all church staff. It is the difference between a large supermarket versus a corner grocery store. It is the difference between a public school classroom versus a Montessori classroom. It is the difference between a pastor-led congregation versus a lay-led congregation.

Growing churches have high expectations of the laity. They not only have high financial and attendance expectations, but also high expectations in growing leaders and their army of volunteers. In general, if a local church expects these things, they will happen.

Conversely, declining churches have low expectations of laity in the programmatic work of the church and high expectations of paid staff persons. New members who join these declining churches with low expectations may unconsciously do so because they are attracted by churches that will not ask them to work hard. Some may have worked hard in their local church leadership ministries in the past, but they are finished with that now. They want to rest and relax. Those who get a payoff in decline want to take it easy and let the staff do it. Conveniently, declining churches seldom reduce staff in proportion to the loss of Sunday morning attendance.

One church with which we consulted has experienced a loss of 600 in Sunday morning worship over the last twenty-five years. They have gone from an average of 1037 to an average of 410. The ordained, lay, support, and maintenance staff have not been cut in proportion to the worship loss. We tell you this not to propose that local churches cut and slash their personnel but to highlight that in declining churches the proportion of paid persons on staff in relation to the church body is much greater than in growing churches. This is common.

At the same time, except for the pastor, staff members still in place tend to be specialists in areas such as children's ministry, youth ministry, or music. It is common for a part-time youth director to only have fifteen to twenty youth in regular attendance, or a children's director to have only forty children active in Sunday school. The answer to growth problems becomes, "We need a full-time person! Our staff members are overworked!" Indeed, most of these staff people do feel overworked because they are trying to "maintain" or manage a program without enough volunteer support—and at a level that isn't in sync with the church's decline.

In local churches that have experienced decline for decades, pastors and programmatic staff are seen as the people who make ministry happen. The staff decides what events in ministry will happen, and the staff is responsible for making the ministry event happen. Laypersons are expected to fund the salaries and ideas of staff, and to volunteer for certain tasks, but they often are excluded from the decision and design stages.

One program staff member was hired to serve a local church that had been in decline for decades. The church gave her the following instructions: "Your primary responsibility is to make these things happen: children's Sunday school, the spring festival, the Christmas pageant, and vacation Bible school."

There was no mention of empowering laity for leadership through training and spiritual growth experiences, and those who are incentivized for decline did not object. There was no mention, beyond lip service, of forming the parents into a team to decide on and implement ministries for children. Working for a church in decline means fewer volunteers, and the volunteers who are available are either overworked or lacking in gifts to get the job done. Most are acclimatized to the low-grade expectation that infects declining churches.

With few laborers available for the tasks she was given, the new staff member tried to do too many things herself. When her teachers wanted the summers off, she taught the Sunday school herself by combining grades one through six. Naturally, fewer and fewer children attended, which truthfully was okay because she and one volunteer couldn't handle thirty-five to forty children. The Sunday school shrank down to a manageable size. When fall came, not all the children returned, and the Sunday school was smaller than years before, and the cycle continued to repeat itself. The new children's ministry director was burned-out in less than three years. She left feeling like a failure as the decline continued uninterrupted. For everyone involved, it was a victory for continued decline and a defeat for the local church's purpose of "making new disciples for Jesus Christ."

REORGANIZE THE WORK OF MINISTRY

Consider these strategies for resisting the temptation to place the work of ministry on clergy and paid staff:

Organize a Bible study around the early church. Examine the structure and model for God's people providing care for one another.

Emphasize that the best way to be fed yourself is by feeding others.

Teach and train staff and lay leaders alike how to mobilize laity for ministry.

Keep staff specialists to a minimum. Work toward having more generalists on the staff. (You can keep the same people if they're good; you're just redefining and broadening the job description. The advantage to this is they have to use more volunteers to get things done.)

Insist on high expectations and accountability from staff and lay leaders.

Empower lay leaders to design and implement new ministries on their own, as long as it fits the vision and purpose of the local congregation.

There are many good ministry resources that organize laity into trained, caring members. Investigate several of them and choose a program to implement. Remember that its success will depend upon both the ability of the staff to let go and the willingness of the staff to empower the volunteers for meaningful ministry experiences. Involve them in leading funerals (you don't have to be ordained to do this). Teach them to pray at the bedside. If your polity permits, let the pastor consecrate the elements, but have the laity take them to the homes of those who are too ill to attend. Trust them. If you micromanage people in this work, they will take it as a sign that:

a) you don't trust them, b) you don't really want them to do it, or c) they aren't doing it as well as you could. They will give up, and you'll say, "I tried, but it didn't work." It is the job of staff and pastors of a local church to empower laity to do ministry.

CHAPTER NINE

The Temptation to Avoid the Hard Work of Assimilation

There is no getting around it. Assimilating new people into the life of a local church is hard work. It takes time, energy, resources, and intentionality. Assimilation of new persons at church takes an attitude adjustment. Assimilation of new persons into a community of faith means doing the hard work of changing a "me first at church" attitude. Assimilation of new persons at church means we give up our demands to be fed and replace them with the desire to feed others. Author Kevin Kloster says it like this:

> One of the difficulties many churches struggle with is the "I want to talk to my friends" syndrome. After a week of not seeing some people from church it's easy to want to spend time talking with them instead of taking a moment to meet and greet

a new person. Often when people say their church is friendly they're talking about this aspect of church. Friendly means I talk with my friends and let them know I care about them, just as they do for me.[1]

Most local church members will recognize the "I want to talk with my friends syndrome." Most will even admit that this behavior isn't helpful for a church that wants to grow. But it is likely that the church member who acknowledges such things, promises to change and be different yet never takes any behavioral steps to be different, is actually receiving a personal payoff for continuing to huddle with his or her friends on Sunday morning.

If there are enough people who perpetuate the "I want to talk to my friends" syndrome on Sunday morning, and they practice this syndrome for years or even decades, your church is virtually guaranteed to continue in a long decline. Kloster describes the damage that can be done:

> Many of us aren't sure what good hospitality looks like, but we know when we haven't felt it. We haven't felt it when we walk into a church and people avoid making eye contact with us. We haven't felt it when people walk right by us as if we didn't exist. We haven't felt it when someone says, "Excuse me, you're sitting in my place." We haven't felt it when people are laughing and talking together but won't include us in the conversation. We haven't felt it when we leave [worship service] and no one even calls to say thank you [for being a guest in worship]. Unfortunately, too many churches think they are friendly but they ignore the guests among them.[2]

If we pay attention to the guests among us, it will limit the time we can talk with our friends before, after, and during church. It takes an intentional effort to say to a friend, "Great to see you. I want to get caught up, but I'm trying to pay attention to new people today. Can I buy you a cup of coffee tomorrow?"

What if the friend says, "No, that won't work, I am swamped this week"? Then people are faced with a dilemma. Do I practice the hospitality of paying attention to new people or recognize I can't "do it all" and meet my needs to talk with my friend in the moment? If enough people choose option two, new people will cease to be a problem for two reasons. First, visitors to your church will be ignored. Once this behavior is repeated week in and week out, there will be fewer visitors to the church. Second, for those who find the work of assimilation too exhausting, their church will remain the same, and this church will become the church that told its adjudicatory representative, "Our vision is to be a church where the pastor leads worship, visits us in the hospital, and is available to do our funeral when we die."

Six to ten new people a year is a manageable number to get to know. If you are part of a declining church but one that is still taking in some new members each year, how many of those new members actually become assimilated into the life of the congregation? The back door of the church is usually open wider than the front! The two declining churches in which we have served still took in between twenty-five to seventy members a year, but death and attrition kept us from ever showing any growth in attendance or membership. Whether a declining church takes in twenty-five or seventy new members a year, only about ten to twelve of them will become fully assimilated into the life and leadership of the congregation. Closing the back door is a key to growing the church, and the way to do it is through small groups. It cannot be stressed enough. Without small groups, a church cannot grow. A church with an average worship attendance of one hundred needs at least twelve different small groups to really thrive.[3]

Some members of your church like to only hang around people they have known for a long time. Some people, out of a preference for keeping things simple, are driven to homogenize complex situations. They live in a black-and-white world, with no gray area.

Others are very comfortable with the old and familiar. They aren't looking for new ideas and practices. The world is changing too fast, and their local church is the last line of defense against a disintegrating culture.

Some people have extraordinary reverence for their local church's aging facilities. Adjustments or alterations to the church plant are more than simple renovations and upkeep. These changes to facilities may elicit a visceral reaction from folks. To put in new flooring or light fixtures may dishonor the saintly member who helped with the design and construction of the original facility. Resistance to these changes may even be evidence of grief that has never been completely processed.

Some people believe their local church's resources are insufficient for their safety and security needs. Asking them to take a risk and trust God to provide resources in the future triggers their anxiety about how, in their mind, there is never enough. The resources that are available are precious and need to be protected.

Local church parlors fit this description. Protectionists sometimes convince the local church trustees to make a rule that no food or drink is allowed in the parlor. The following is a recent conversation between a women's group member and the organizer of a going-away party for a local church staff member.

"How are you going to set the tables?" the women's group leader asked.

"We were planning on using the round tables with a table covering and candles," the organizer said cautiously.

"What kind of table coverings did you have in mind?"

"We were going to use those round ones in the closet over there."

"Those are the church women's group tablecloths," the group leader reported.

"I know; they look nice. We want the reception to be nice."

"I suppose it would be all right to use them," the women's group leader hesitated, "if you didn't put them out until right before the event and kept children from drinking juice at the tables."

"Never mind," the organizer decided. "We'll just go with cut paper for table coverings. We don't want to risk harming the group's tablecloths."

Where did we get the idea that our tablecloths were more important than practicing hospitality? If the church grows, there will be more demands on the tablecloths. If the church declines, then the guarantee will be that the tablecloths will either (a) seldom be used or (b) used under supervision that gives them the best chance at long life and keeping them looking nice.

Remember plastic couch coverings? Some rooms—some churches—are too perfect to actually use.

Last, some people aren't committee people. They like to do things themselves, their way, and in their own time. To meet with others and come to a group decision is against their nature. They may not be good at playing well with others.

If you see yourself in descriptions inside this section, you may be someone who is ambivalent about the decline at your local church. You are not in favor of decline, but you are unwilling to work hard to grow. Growth will be unsettling for you, and your world has a better chance to maintain stability and comfort if the church stays the same. You may even experience more personal security in decline. Growth might make things spin out of control.

Growth brings unwanted stress to persons who have incentives for the local church to decline. Strangers force us to make adjustments and alterations to our facilities, our ministries, our worship, and our administration.

PRACTICE RADICAL HOSPITALITY

This incentive can only be changed with great intentionality. If someone is coming over to your house, there are certain things you are going to do to make them feel welcome and comfortable. Consider this "to do" list for preparing a home for company:

Clean the place up. Put things away that are scattered about. Wash dishes, wipe off the countertops, sweep the floor, and so on.

Prepare something to eat. If it is dinnertime, cook a meal. Food needs to be fresh and presentation makes a difference, so maybe use the nice plates and cloth napkins.

If it isn't dinnertime, prepare light snacks or appetizers.

Offer a beverage of choice.

Since where people sit is important, position bar stools in the breakfast nook while finishing food preparation, then move to the living room after the meal.

Practice your best listening skills in preparation for narratives from your guests.

The list is endless. The goal is to welcome friends, family, and new guests in a way that communicates radical hospitality. It is time that we outdid each other in practicing radical hospitality at our local churches. Because there will always be some members of our congregation not looking for new faces and not willing to do the hard work of hospitality, we have to make this a priority. Every Sunday, we invite guests to our church home. Let's do it right. Here are some things we can do each Sunday:

Spruce up the outside. Mow lawns, trim landscaping, make restrooms spotless, and even touch up fresh paint when possible (even people with incentives for the church to be smaller might pitch in here!).

Prepare something to eat. Make snacks of some kind, and not just for the group that has been meeting together for twenty-five or thirty years, but snacks for everyone. Place them out in places where every guest will have access to them. Make sure there is a balance between more healthy and less healthy snacks. Be generous with portions.

Make good decaf and regular coffee. This is a Starbucks world, and hospitality means providing the best. Serve a high-quality blend of coffee. Provide juice, tea, or lemonade for kids and those who don't drink coffee.

Have a "connections" table where people can gather. Use this as "information central."

Have all ushers and greeters trained in radical hospitality. Insist they begin with a smile.

Practice the "hand off." If you are the first one to meet a newcomer, look for another member who is close in age and life stage as the newcomer and hand off the hospitality function to that other member.

Get as much information as possible from the newcomer, written and verbal. Make sure the registration pads that record attendance retrieve all the information necessary for making connections.

Have a system of post-worship contact. Initiate email, telephone, and doorstep visits to the newcomer's home, possibly even taking a gift from the church. Let the laity decide what to do because they are the ones who will be doing it! Start small; grow in scope.

With repeat visitors, work hard to connect them to existing small groups. If the newcomers' needs are not represented by an existing small group, think about starting a new group.

Constantly evaluate and reevaluate the effectiveness of your hospitality efforts. Use a "secret Sunday morning visitor" from the outside to identify your hospitality blind spots.

The goal is to make newcomers feel as though they are the most important person in the world for that Sunday morning. If they feel that radical hospitality from the outset, and you are willing to listen closely to their story, a relationship will likely develop.

Make space for others by having an extra chair, more refreshments, an additional study book, a warm smile, and a welcome handshake. Here are a few extra tips:

Have three or four questions ready for the one who is a stranger to you. "Where are you from?" "What do you like to do?" "What is your church background?"

Practice patience when things appear chaotic or intrusive.

Practice patience as it will take some time for monetary resources to catch up with new growth.

Work hard at radical hospitality and assimilation.

PART IV
The Need
for Stability

I Liked It Better the Way It Used to Be . . . Consider the simi-
larities between congregational and personal life. For many
years, we welcome life changes: childhood, adolescence, mat-
uration, graduation, careers, marriage, and children of our own.
But when we face failure, middle age, illness, and loss, we feel the
need for stability in the sea of change.

Growth is natural in the beginning years of a church's life. Par-
ticipants anticipate and celebrate milestones like reaching a certain number of members, finishing a new building, burning the
mortgage, or building a large staff. Churches could have an indef-
inite shelf life, yet few of them do.

Weary from storms and setbacks, we yearn for one thing to stay the same in life, and often, we want the church to be that one thing. Most churches kindly oblige. Eventually, our grand architecture outlasts our congregational vitality and becomes a bewildering legacy of beauty in modern life.

WE WILL BE HERE LONG AFTER YOU ARE GONE!

New people bring change. New people bring chaos. New people bring surprises that can be disruptive. For those who demand order, routine, and the dependability of sameness, one major temptation for them is to impose that need upon the church. Keeping familiar programs, leaders, and worship styles is paramount.

The first two years for pastors are usually spent getting "the lay of the land." It takes time to develop relationships and learn about a church's history. Most pastors try to discover which leaders will help the church grow and move forward. Some current leaders who are resistant to change will feel pressure to behave in new ways. If they are capable of doing so, there may be a smooth leadership transition, but for those who are not capable, anxiety grows about the impending loss of stability. The slightest changes seem monumental to them. Resistance can begin simply from alternating tunes for the doxology. It is better for these anxious leaders if the turnstile of pastors keeps turning. No new vision and keeping the "same old, same old" will mean there is less danger of "our church turning into one of those new, modern-type churches with screens, guitars, and pastors wearing jeans," as one church member told us.

Strange as it may seem, there is one systemic change that will have enormous payoffs for those who wish for things at their local church to stay the same: change pastors. To prevent changes in the local church, it is essential that there is frequent pastoral change in that church. It is well documented that healthy, thriving, and growing churches, more often than declining churches, have long-term pastorates. Declining churches have a carousel approach to pastoral leadership. Many declining and dying churches have two-year or three-year pastorates. Here is a typical cycle:

For the first two years of any appointment or call, the pastor gets to know the "lay of the land," which means developing relationships and discovering which leaders will help the local church move forward. Those church members who are incentivized for decline, who are resistant to change, will feel the pressure to behave in new ways. If those historically resistant to change are capable of changing, there may be a smooth transition. But for those who are not capable, anxiety will grow about losing their current influence through their formal or informal leadership positions. It is better for these anxious leaders if the turnstile of pastors keeps turning. In constant turnover, there is great difficulty articulating new vision and not enough time to build wide consensus around a new vision with more forward-thinking members. No new vision and the maintenance of "same old, same old" will mean there is little danger of being ousted.

It isn't difficult to identify those who see a change in pastoral leadership as a way to keep change away from the local church. They may say things like:

"I hope the next pastor will be better than the last one."

"I love our church. I just wish we could find a pastor who would recognize how great our church has always been."

"We were here when that pastor came, and we will be here long after she is gone."

One clergy colleague who was in a position of administrative oversight for forty-plus churches met with a powerful layman whose church had been in decline for decades. This layman was quite unhappy with his current pastor and griped to anyone who would listen that "he isn't right for our church." Our colleague shared that the church had frequently changed pastors, and usually at this particular layman's instigation. The reasons for each change varied, but the consistent bottom line was that no pastor measured up to what the church needed. Meanwhile, the church continued to decline, and none of the pastors in this revolving door had enough time to gain traction with a new vision. Length of pastoral tenure is one of the keys to overall vitality, attendance growth, membership growth, and increased engagement of the church as a whole.[1]

Short-term pastorates of less than five years are part of a winning formula to limit change and keep a greater portion of power in the hands of those who have an incentive for decline. With deep sighs and pleas to those in authority, these leaders will say in one breath, "I do hope the next pastor is better than the last one!" while simultaneously warning all who dare enter their pulpits, "We never have done it that way and don't want to start it now!"

CHAPTER TEN

The Temptation to
Play It Safe

S ome lay folks would favor building a symbolic, if not literal, gate around their worship area and small group life. Some want to enforce a dress code for worship. Laypersons with a high need for safety and security are likely drawn by the temptation to play it safe. As churches decline, it becomes easier to exercise control.

In preaching a series on Revelation in one local church, we talked of our changing world and the need for openness to diversity within the church. One congregational lay leader sent the following in an email response:

> The 20% of your sermon Sunday that was devoted to Revelations was excellent. Your presentation was informative, and the material tied together well. The remaining portion of your message, which dealt with societal change, was not so well received. No one would disagree that society has changed in the past 50 years, but, in the opinion of many of us, not for the better. We are a coarser, crasser, more crude, less civil society now than we

were then. The way people dress reflects how they think about themselves and, to a large degree, how they act. Rather than the church saying, "here is our standard, and our expectation is that you will live up to it," the preferred path has been for the church to flow with the societal norms of the moment. The majority of the 11:00 service is comprised of those of us who are older, who have attended church for a number of years, dress respectfully and appropriately for worship services, and are not particularly open to hearing chastisement for that point of view.

That last sentence tells it all. The layperson who wrote this email may not realize he believes he holds the definition of all things respectful and appropriate. The clear assumption is that, in his mind, every other participant in the life of the church needs to adhere to his notion of what respectful and appropriate might be. To fail to do so means, at least, civility cannot be maintained and, at most, the participant is an affront to God and Jesus Christ.

It doesn't matter what kind of inclusion statement we write in our Sunday bulletins. The message is clear: Persons who dress like us, think like us, have a similar worldview as us, hold sacred what we hold sacred, worship in the same style and form as us, look like us, and act like us are welcome to come and join us. Great diversity isn't welcome here.

Uninterrupted local church decline is the best way to ensure long-running homogeneity. We say "the best way" because there are churches that have maintained a high level of homogeneity and have evidenced significant growth in the past. Years ago Fuller Seminary identified a church growth principle called the Homogeneous Unit Principle (HUP), which states that the less people are required to change racial, linguistic, or class barriers, the more likely people are to become followers of Christ. While homogeneity is seen less favorably in today's multicultural settings, many churches assume that effective ministry targets homogeneous groups. Laypersons who live by their incentive for local church decline will use the homogeneity principle to limit the profile of what constitutes a desirable new member. The more qualifiers for desirability, the fewer new members. If there are no new members, normal attrition through transfers and death will decline the church. The persons whose self-interest is served through continued decline are protecting what is valuable to them and strengthening their place in the community.

CHANGE IS DISRUPTIVE AND DECLINING CHURCHES FACE LESS CHANGE

It is sad but true that change has become the enemy of most church members in the last forty years. We did a very informal survey of United Methodist pastors and lay leaders in Arizona in 2010. An even 50 percent didn't believe in the need for change within our local churches. That figure isn't from the pews. It is from our leaders.

"I'm not opposed to trying new things, but don't you think the new guy should go slowly with all these changes in order to bring everyone along?"

"I've never seen so much dissension in my beloved church (which has been in decline for twenty-five years)!"

These comments rarely appear as a full frontal assault. They more often surface as fomentations of discontent after the fact. The following scenario occurred at a gathering of the trustees. An AA group had petitioned the church to use a classroom for their weekly meetings.

"We have been talking for over an hour about having the AA group meet in our building. I want to make sure that all have had a chance to share their feelings. This is very important if we are to present a unified front before the congregation. Is there anyone here who has some last words about this subject, negative or positive, before we put it to a vote?" (silence)

"Anyone at all?" (more silence)

"Then let's proceed with a vote. All those in favor of granting the AA group access once a week in room 114 signify by saying 'Aye.' Those opposed?" (silence)

"Then it is decided."

After the meeting, one long-term member who said nothing during the entire trustees meeting received a call from another long-term member who was not a trustee.

"What is this I hear about a bunch of alcoholics coming to take over our building?"

"Yeah, I'm pretty upset about it too. Those are not the kind of people we want associated with our church."

"Didn't anyone speak out against it?"

"I tried to, but nobody would listen. I think the pastor called several people before the meeting and lobbied for this decision, but I can't be sure."

"I am afraid this is going to tear our church apart."

"It very well could do just that. I'm sure others feel the same way. It seems such a shame to have all this controversy. People are so upset now that we have this new pastor."

All this is said after the meeting, a meeting where the primary sower of discontent didn't speak one word. This kind of after-meeting conversation is typical and helpful to those who wish to keep rotating pastors. It keeps anxiety high and foments discontent with leadership. It is a way to insure the local church will continue in decline.

New faces for Jesus Christ also create disruptions to the local church's administrative life. When new people begin to worship regularly at a local church and commit themselves to the responsibilities of membership, many have leadership gifts and are looking for a place to exercise those gifts. Programmatic change can throw a disruption into family life that has become familiar and comfortable. When we were appointed to serve at First United Methodist Church of Phoenix, we quickly learned three things:

There were three worship services with a combined Sunday morning worship average of a little more than four hundred.

The first worship service was a duplicate of the last worship service and averaged less than forty in weekly attendance.

There was no designated church school hour on Sunday morning.

The children's Sunday school program took place at nine thirty. This was the same time as the contemporary worship service in the sanctuary. Implementing what had been discussed for years, the worship committee voted to eliminate the earlier classic worship service and move the contemporary service to the nine a.m. hour. This made the ten a.m. hour available for a "womb-to-tomb" Sunday school program.

One leader of the church asked us, "And why we are doing this?"

"The worship committee and the council voted to do this so everyone in the family would be able to attend a Sunday school class, children and adults alike."

"But our family was comfortable with the past format. We like going to church, and our kids like going to Sunday school. Now, they have to sit in church with us, and that is disruptive. Plus, they aren't going to be able to attend Sunday school. This won't work for us."

"Well, we would be glad to explore alternatives for kids who aren't used to attending worship. With your help we could perhaps have a children's church program as a transitional piece in having kids become more acclimated to sitting through worship. There are other things we can do in the contemporary service to make it more child-friendly."

"But what are my wife and I supposed to do while the kids are in Sunday school class from ten to eleven o'clock?"

"You both could attend an adult class."

"But I don't like any of the adult classes," he said. (Honestly, there were only two in operation, with an average class membership age of sixty-eight.)

"Agreed; we need to build up some choices. We could talk about starting a new class with persons your same age and family configuration," we responded, hoping this conversation would be the start of building something new and exciting.

(Long pause) "But I can't go to both worship and Sunday school. I don't have two hours per week to give to the church."

This wasn't an exploratory member, a seeker, someone who was testing the waters to see if the practice of our Christian faith was for him. This was an elected leader in the church. Change in programming is disruptive, but when the chair of a power committee in the church confesses he doesn't have two hours per week to give to his local church, that is destructive to the stated purpose of the local church making new disciples for Jesus Christ. A church cannot make disciples in one hour per week.

If a person gets elected to a visible leadership position, and he or she is resistant to giving any more than one hour per week to a journey in Christian life, then there is a problem. If this leader enjoys the benefits of his leadership position—recognition, power, significant voice in the decisions of the local church—and he perceives a threat from a changing local church culture, then he will likely join the ranks of those who succumb to temptations for decline. Due to the fact that he is unwilling to meet the more demanding expectations of leadership in a growing church, there is apparently payoff for him when the church continues to decline.

LAITY, MAKE YOUR CHURCH THE BEST PLACE TO WORK

One cure for the need for stability is to make the church a great place to work. Conventional wisdom says that years four through seven of a pastor's leadership are the most productive. Lay leaders, what can a church do to hang on to a good pastor as long as possible? Create conditions that make him or her want to stay:

Pay him or her well.

Encourage creativity.

Encourage one another to tithe; money messages are often much better coming from another member than from clergy.

Treat the pastor as a spiritual leader.

Be a full partner in ministry.

Limit the number of meetings the pastor is expected to attend to an average of one night a week; meetings don't grow churches, ministry does.

If housing is provided, make sure it is up to the standards of the average home in the church's membership.

Fund the pastor's continuing education needs.

Insist the pastor take one full day off during the Monday-through-Friday week.

Grant paid sabbatical leaves for up to three months every seven years.

If you are in a rural area or a small town, look for someone who grew up in that culture and appreciates the life small communities can offer.

Be up front and ask the pastor how long she or he will stay. You have the right to ask for a commitment.

PASTORS, HONESTLY EVALUATE YOUR POSITION

Pastors, you are the other half of this equation. Let's face it: If you accept a call or an appointment to a church you don't really want, you are being unfair to yourself and the congregation. Sure, you can think it's only temporary, but is that fair to you or to the church? Is that what God wants? If you fail to find an opportunity for the kind of church you are looking for, maybe God is trying to tell you to reexamine your ministry perspective. If you want to serve a large church, maybe you're not ready for that; accept a staff position. Maybe you only want to serve in a specific geographical area (like a big city, or only where your spouse is already employed). These aren't bad things, but you are limiting yourself. So, to compensate, open up your heart to a broader range of possibilities instead of taking a church you don't want with an unspoken plan of moving as quickly as you can. Longer pastorates require an honest, soul-searching process between you, God, and the ministry possibility.

Speak honestly about what it would take for you to have a long-term commitment with the congregation. It is a covenantal relationship, but the covenant begins with good communication. Don't be coy; it starts with you. Here are some steps you can take:

If you are already in a position, you are right if you believe that they don't understand your job. Tell them about it—at length. Don't pretend you can do everything, or that you are good at all the tasks of ministry. No one is.

Taking care of yourself is up to you. No one can make you do it, and you know that. If you don't take your day off seriously, no one else will either. If your own spiritual growth isn't paramount to you, the congregation won't think it's important either.

If you are unhappy and want to move because your church isn't involved enough in mission, lead them. If they aren't passionate enough in worship, show them your passion. If there is a lack of spiritual maturity or theological depth, take them there yourself. If the church is too small, grow it. In other words, make your church a place you can't bear to leave.

If there isn't enough financial support, make sure you tithe yourself and be open about it; expect the staff to tithe as well. If the staff leaders don't, why should the congregation?

Try putting aside your understandable desire to climb the ladder. Trust God that under your leadership, the church you pastor can and will transform the lives of countless persons God sends your way. This is enough. If God wants you to shepherd a mega-flock, the possibilities and opportunities will find you; you don't have to seek them out or lay out a career path.

Epilogue

Moving Forward: How to Resist the Temptations of Church

I f we are to revitalize churches and experience church growth, then we must recognize these temptations toward decline. It is difficult for the laypersons described here to embrace church growth. Some will be persuaded through biblical reminders such as the Great Commission in Matthew 28. However, others will never be positive about the work of growing their local church. As leaders in the revitalization task, we need to listen to their concerns, measure the effect of those concerns on others, yet stay focused on the vision of growing the church—no exceptions.

After identifying all ten temptations, all the ways that our "me first" thinking poisons our local churches, the question becomes, What do we do? How do we transform or transcend active local church leaders who experience an incentive in continuing church decline?

1. Practice the Principle of Alignment. Make Sure All Your Ministries Fulfill Your Primary Purpose of Making New Disciples. If a Ministry Cannot Do that, Change it.

New ideas take us out of our ruts. New ideas can bring new energy that otherwise would be hard to generate. One older, well-established church put on a fall festival for years. The festival was held in the church parking lot. It had game booths, a cakewalk, pony rides, hot dogs, hamburgers, and a dunking booth. In the last two years, it became increasingly difficult to recruit volunteers to help set up or tear down. In the last year, no one wanted to help with any of it, even the games.

During a weekly staff meeting the children's coordinator said, "We need to talk about the fall festival." Right away everyone could feel the energy drain out of the room. Rather than a celebration, the fall festival had turned into a chore.

Someone asked the unthinkable. "What if we didn't have a fall festival this year? What if we did something else instead? It would still be a church-wide thing, but it would be new, fresh, and alive. What if we did something like that?"

Eyes lit up, smiles came back to faces, and wheels started turning inside heads. Everyone was ready for something different. That year, they tried a big project around Christmastime that was well received by the whole church and brought lots of new people to their local church campus. There was great energy in this new effort. The next year, someone asked, "Are we ready to repeat our new all-church Christmastime celebration this year? We had lots of participation last year, and people reported they really loved it!"

"I've talked with a bunch of folks, and you are right—people loved it," responded another staff member, "but that was last year, and this is a new year. I feel that we should gather key lay leadership around the table and brainstorm what other ideas are out there for us to do."

There was agreement all around, and the wheels were set in motion for a new kind of excitement in a new ministry to reach new people.

2. Rely on Your Own Human Resources Instead of Hiring Outside Help. Stay Flexible!

For most churches driven to revitalization, money is tight. Healthy, growing churches make liberal use of human resources at their disposal as opposed to declining churches, which lean on monetary resources. Remember the movie *Pay It Forward?* The young protagonist didn't have much in the way of financial resources, but he tapped into an abundant human resource to do good. Healthy churches are like that. Healthy churches activate the laity for innovative and exciting ministries driven by the human resource of Christian disciples in the local church.

A local church that was in decline for decades wanted to try something new. They wanted to get the word out that, not only were they occupying the block, they were alive and exciting! Someone contacted a marketing group and was put in touch with a business that distributed door hangers in targeted neighborhoods. How much would it cost to distribute door hangers to the 5,000 homes within their three-mile radius? $10,000. The leadership group of that local church was discouraged.

"We don't have $10,000!" a church leader said out loud, pushing the wind out of everyone's sails in the room, except one.

"Maybe not," the one answered, "but there are ten of us in this room. What if each of us were to recruit five people who were able to then recruit five more people? What if those 250 people would meet on one Saturday morning for a breakfast and inspirational rally? What if after breakfast and the rally everyone took enough door hangers to distribute in their neighborhood—just one block, both sides of the street? What if one or two persons on their street were willing to stop and talk about church, faith, and how connected or disconnected they felt from God? What if just one household per block would accept a personal invitation from that neighbor to attend church this next month? That would be better than some anonymous door hanger, and it would give us a great Saturday morning celebration and save us $10,000 all at once."

3. Transforming People without Their Knowledge and Permission Is Pretty Much Impossible.

We can, however, seek and receive agreement to some basic principles, such as all ministries and programs must somehow further the overall purpose of making new disciples for Jesus Christ. That way, whenever an old program is evaluated or a new program is proposed, these two questions come first:

How will this new thing bring new faces to our church?

How will we connect long-time members and friends to the new people who come?

Above all, remember that whatever your local church has is enough to do what God wants. Churches in desperate need of revitalization can begin to grow again. Some of those who carry incentives for decline will be redirected by embracing again, or maybe for the first time, the local church purpose of connecting new faces to Jesus Christ. But even if people who find personal advantage in their local church's decline never come around, the purpose of our local churches does not change. We must work around them.

We can put those who have incentive for decline to work on worthy projects such as leading an effort to record the local church history, recording the faces and stories of long-time members for projected image, keeping up the beloved church campus, and soliciting older members for designated and undesignated gifts to the local church foundation. They can lead the effort to honor the church's history without attempting to stifle the dreams and visions of leaders hungry to make new disciples for Jesus Christ.

Renovations, remodels, and new buildings can be fun projects and create excitement within the local church as well. Many times church members and friends who have nonverbal gifts will receive significant affirmations as they lead these projects. It is important to find ways to lift up and celebrate the contributions of those who bring non-verbal gifts to your local church. Those with verbal gifts, such as public prayers, moderating and leading meetings, scripture reading, and witnessing in worship, for the most part, receive more affirmations than those whose primary gifts are nonverbal. Find a way to praise every gift that comes to the church.

RECOGNIZE AND NAME THE FEAR

We have left the fear factor for last, because underneath and woven through all other temptations is fear. Fear is crippling. It causes us to do things we would not otherwise consider. There is no question we live in fearful times, and the projections are that these times will continue in the decade to come. After Jesus' death, the first disciples must have been terrified as they gathered behind locked doors in the upper room. Yet the presence of the risen Christ emboldened them to step beyond their fear into a world that was every bit as threatening to them, if not more so, than ours is to us. Within the heart of the church is the power to confront fears that cripple human life and dignity.

On our midday visit to an aging downtown church we tried the only visible door and found it locked. We were surprised, since we had an appointment and were expected. Looking around, we saw a bell ten feet from the door and rang that bell.

A disembodied voice asked, "Welcome. May I help you?"

"We have an appointment with the pastor. How do we get inside?"

"I will buzz you in. Once you get inside, come up the steps and walk to the end of the hall and you will find our offices on the left."

Immediately, the voice disappeared and a buzzer went off. Before we could get to the handle to open the door, the sound of the buzzer had stopped. Trying the door and finding it still locked, we returned to the bell and rang it again.

"Welcome to the church. May I help you?"

"Yes, I spoke with you just a moment ago. We have an appointment, and I didn't get to the door when it was unlocked. Would you please try again?"

"Yes, I will buzz you in. Once you get inside, come up the steps and walk to the end of the hall and you will find our offices on the left."

This time, as soon as the buzzer sounded, we hurried to pull on the door. It wouldn't open. Simultaneously, we realized it must be the second set of double doors, not the set closest to the doorbell and speakers. But the race to that door was too late. The buzzer had stopped, and both doors were still locked. We looked at each other, feeling like characters in a slapstick movie or a *Candid Camera* video. We returned to the bell and rang it for the third time.

"Welcome to the church; may I help you?"

"Us again. We missed the simultaneous buzzer and door handle thing again."

"I will buzz you in. Once you get inside, come up the steps and walk to the end of the hall and you will find our offices on the left."

On this last attempt, we found the correct door handle and pulled the door open when the buzzer sounded. As we walked into the hallway and started up the steps, we saw a security camera that had likely recorded our every amusing move. Entering into the church office, we shared our surprise and frustration in a light-handed way. "It is easier to make entry into a minimum security prison than it is to gain access to this local church and sanctuary."

The receptionist was polite and gracious as she offered an explanation. Fifteen years ago, there was a disturbing incident at the church. An associate pastor was attempting to minister to a man who happened to be homeless, and that man was also untreated in his mental illness. One afternoon, the man from the streets attacked the associate pastor inside the church with a typewriter. Although physically the pastor was fine, emotionally he had been shaken. More shaken was the congregation, who believed the whole downtown area had become unsafe. The buzzer and security camera were installed after that. (In truth, the downtown area was a popular tourist area in that city, and it had the lowest crime rate of all the city's sectors.) Safety and security became the first order of business for this local church, in spite of a church marketing slogan: "Open hearts, open minds, open doors."

We believe there is a correlation between erecting more gates and installing more locks and decline. The greater the fear among the congregants, the more lockdown security is put in place. The more lockdown security is in place, the more decline for the local church. People who believe everything is going to hell are motivated to fan the fear. People who fan the fear feed the local church's decline.

Ironically, the "payoff" in place was just an illusion of security. It was only an illusion because, in truth, everyone who came to the front doors was buzzed in. Another hallway and two staircases fed off the main hallway to the offices. Anyone entering could easily have wandered off and hidden anywhere inside the 15,000-square-foot building.

It's as if we still think we live in a wagon train. Remember the old Westerns when the wagon train was under attack? The wagon train leader would yell out instructions, "Circle the wagons!" Hearing this message, those driving the wagons would arrange them in a tight circle, making a defensive position to keep safe within the circle while holding off the enemy forces trying to do harm from the outside. The church laypersons who circle the wagons believe and often proclaim out loud to anyone who will listen, "The world (or church) is going to hell in a handbasket."

We are not suggesting that evil and destruction are not part of our modern world. The church must be realistic, and the world can be scary. Teenagers used to get sent to the principal for wearing their hair over their collars and their skirts too short. Today's teenagers walk down the street with underwear in clear view. Worse, dogs and security guards roam high school hallways, removing drugs and weapons.

A friend reports that her elementary-school-age niece and nephews ride the bus to school every day. The school system requires a parent or a guardian to bring children to the bus stop and wait with them until the bus driver picks the child up. Furthermore, it is the case that, for this school district, if a parent or guardian isn't waiting for that child at the bus stop when the bus returns, then the driver is instructed not to let the child off the bus but to return that child to the school for parents to pick them up from the elementary school office.

It is a new world, an uncertain world. Some folks choose to live in a gated community to keep the world out. In less affluent neighborhoods, where gates, security guards, and doormen are not available, many houses have bars covering the windows and doors of their homes. Airport security has tightened, the faces of missing children are displayed on milk cartons, and childcare workers are fingerprinted and required to undergo a background check. We do not suggest that appropriate precautions be ignored.

Yet broadcast descriptions of violence outpace actual statistics, and the level of fear that we have for personal safety and local church safety is out of proportion to the threat. This fear level is paralyzing many churches.

HOW CAN THE CYCLE OF FEAR BE BROKEN?

Expose the illusion of security; deal with the underlying fear of change.

Encourage risk taking.

The aging downtown church with more protection than Fort Knox was paying a high price for its supposed security. What was it costing them in terms of their neighbors and visitors who came calling? Eventually, we challenged the need to "circle the wagons" by recalling their rich history of risk taking. We reminded them of a history that included giving sanctuary to persons of Japanese descent during World War II, and how they had reached out in the past to servicemen who came in off the streets, and to young women with problem pregnancies, all of which were risky business.

Eventually the church's offices were moved up front, where everyone could see through glass doors that no longer had to stay locked all day. Hidden emergency buzzers were installed under the desks to reassure and create feelings of real safety. Within a few years the congregation had a thriving ministry to the people of that city who found themselves homeless. The local church was revitalized through inclusiveness of the least, the last, and the lost. To be sure, every member didn't embrace this new identity. Some left, but more were attracted by the church's authenticity and hands-on mission.

CHANGE THE CULTURE

Our declining churches are needy churches and fearful churches. Not at a conscious level perhaps, but insistence that the church's life be bent to the needs of the individual is active in every dying congregation. In the truest sense of the word, these churches have become preference-centered churches, not purpose-centered churches. The world does not take our declining local churches seriously precisely because they are driven by the personal preferences of their members rather than the mission of Christ in our world. Mainline denominations, which used to have power in our culture, are now seen as irrelevant to public policy and practice and are thereby irrelevant as a challenging voice of transformation.

Historically, the church has tried to bring about change in our members through two primary pathways: fear and guilt. On one hand, we have preached eternal damnation for those who don't follow the teachings of Christ. A small church signboard on a free-way between two cities in south Texas carried this succinct message of fear to all who passed by: "Get Right or Get Left!" This local church was small and suffering from decline. Obviously, this message didn't produce the desired result of a growing, thriving community of faith. There are as many dying fundamentalist churches as there are dying moderate and liberal ones. The threat of hell won't bring about a change in our local churches; those days are gone and most of us are glad.

On the other hand, when fear didn't work, guilt did. The image of Jesus hanging on a cross, dying for us, was used to bring us into line with his teachings. When the movie *The Passion of the Christ* came out, we saw a resurgence in the effectiveness of this tactic, but it faded with the season. Whether or not you believe fear and guilt are appropriate methods to change the church doesn't really matter anymore. They simply don't work in the postmodern world.

In fact, everything we know about church, from how to preach a sermon to how to run a meeting, is undergoing a shift. We need something else if we are to do battle with the temptations of church.

What are twenty-first-century seekers or believers looking for, if not heaven and guilt relief? Fortunately, they are looking for exactly what it is that the church is best equipped to offer. They are looking for what lies at the heart of the gospel: meaning, hope, and community. We can change if we turn from incentives of decline back to the heart of what Christ brings to our world.

THE CHRISTIAN FAITH
DEFINES MEANING

No one wants to be irrelevant. Many people come to church in their quest for meaning. The declining church represents finding meaning through a combination of personal power, caring, affirmation, and stability. The transformational church, on the other hand, guides people to meaning through finding joy, sharing of the heart, and self-giving through the demonstration of justice, love, and mercy.

First, believe that your congregation truly wants to live inside a culture of finding joy in today rather than living in the fear of tomorrow. Former Asbury Theological Seminary president Maxie Dunnam has said, "People whose [need] is for security—and that [need] turns them into miserly people—are people who rob themselves of joy today because of their fear of tomorrow." In Luke Jesus cautions us:

> Then he said to them, "Watch out! Be on your guard against all kinds of greed; a man's life does not consist in the abundance of his possessions."

And he told them this parable: "The ground of a certain rich man produced a good crop. He thought to himself, 'What shall I do? I have no place to store my crops.'

"Then he said, 'This is what I'll do. I will tear down my barns and build bigger ones, and there I will store all my grain and my goods. And I'll say to myself, "You have plenty of good things laid up for many years. Take life easy; eat, drink and be merry."'" (Luke 12:15-20 NIV)

We can see our current fear of tomorrow as we build our modern-day barns with the proliferation of storage units, as we accumulate more and more possessions. We try to safeguard today against an uncertain future. Finding joy in today means taking some risks in life! Karen worked with the local church foundation at one church we served. This church had an entire floor devoted to storage, including financial records and bulletins going back to the 1950s. They had 4.5 million dollars in foundation assets, but the fear of tomorrow drove them to build that foundation for a "rainy day" and store everything they owned so it could be used sometime in the future when the church was full again. Karen asked them to imagine with her that Jesus returned to our church and went on a tour with us through our building.

As Jesus walked through an entire unused floor, he asked what we did with this space, and we said, "We're saving it for when we're growing again. This chair was given by Mrs. Jones, and this sofa was a gift from Judge Smith."

"Are there no needs in downtown right now? Does no one you know need this space? Perhaps I can give it to someone else, and they will know how to use it," Jesus said.

When we returned to the offices, Jesus said, "And your millions of dollars? That's a beautiful spirit of giving. What are you doing with that?"

"We're saving that, too, Jesus, for that 'rainy day.' It's all for you, Jesus."

Karen said to the foundation, "What would he say to us? 'Well done, good and faithful servant?' Really? What does Jesus mean in Matthew 6?"

> "Therefore I tell you, do not worry about your life, what you will eat or drink; or about your body, what you will wear. Is not life more important than food, and the body more than clothes? Look at the birds of the air; they do not sow or reap or store away in barns, and yet your heavenly Father feeds them. Are you not much more valuable than they? Who of you by worrying can add a single hour to his life?" (Matthew 6:25-27 NIV)

Gradually, through faith and study, preaching and teaching, the church moved into the joy of today, as they began to connect to their neighborhood. That unused floor of the church eventually became a location of ministry for the least, the last, and the lost. The fear of tomorrow paralyzes, and the joy of today liberates. Only the gospel can change the culture and free us from old patterns. Move the church culture from internal to external, preference-driven to purpose-centered, and emphasize the payoff of finding meaning in self-giving as a life worth living.

> And whoever does not take up the cross and follow me is not worthy of me. Those who find their life will lose it, and those who lose their life for my sake will find it.
> "Whoever welcomes you welcomes me, and whoever welcomes me welcomes the one who sent me." (Matt 10:38-40)

THE CHRISTIAN FAITH DEFINES COMMUNITY

Isolation and loneliness continue to plague American society. The popularity of Facebook speaks to the desire to connect with others; it just isn't equipped to do it at a deep and meaningful level;

the church is. In fact, the church is uniquely gifted to be that connecting glue in and among persons, at a deep level and in meaningful ways.

To establish a culture of joy for today, then, each individual church person needs to repeat the mantra, "It is not about me!" It is about the least, the last, and the lost. It is about the other. It is about loving the unlovable. It is about self-giving and the adventure of living outside our comfort zones. There we will find our meaning and purpose. The church is still called to lead our culture through embodiment of this "kingdom-of-God-life." The church is looking for ways to resist the ten "me first" temptations, and this begins when church folks treat each other with mutual dignity and respect. They must also share a common vision and the demonstration of justice, love, and mercy.

If we practice the joy of today, and if we live inside self-giving, we will find ourselves in a culture of love and mercy. Consider those persons who have become famous because they lived inside the demonstration of justice, love, and mercy: Martin Luther King, Jr., Mohandas Gandhi, Nelson Mandela, and Mother Teresa. Now consider the not-so-famous names of persons in the local church who lived as persons of justice, love, and mercy. A Sunday school teacher? A pastor? A playful layperson who lived in the joy of that day, who always had time for coffee with strangers or time to listen to the unloved? This is a life that transforms the church and world. Ironically, power and influence flow naturally to such persons, even as their behaviors are not motivated by power and influence.

A laywoman, deep inside the culture of sacrificial giving, heard that a friend of a friend needed a kidney but was unlikely to find a match because of his rare blood type. This young laywoman was a single mom with modest resources, yet she shared the stranger's blood type. From the moment she heard the story, she consulted her pastor and began praying for God's will to be revealed to her.

In the end, she made the decision to give one of her kidneys to this stranger because she was a follower of Jesus. Her six-year-old son was being trained about how to act in this culture of self-giving and self-sacrifice. He was excited and volunteered one of his own kidneys. Mom smiled. Her son was growing into the person Jesus had created him to be. After surgery and recovery, this mom achieved recognition, power, and affirmation from her community of faith. She didn't look for this payoff, yet it came to her because she demonstrated justice, love, and mercy for a stranger.

THE CHRISTIAN FAITH DEFINES HOPE

If real meaning is found in self-giving, and true community is found in the body of Christ, what is our hope? The concentration of wealth in the hands of a few continues, along with the depletion of our natural resources and the escalation of violence all over the world. For some, hope lies in the triumphant return of Christ, who will slay our foes and prove us right. This is what the religious establishment of Jesus' day thought too. Yet the words of Jesus and the Hebrew Scriptures point us to another hope, and this is the hope which will lead us into God's intended future: "Thy kingdom come, thy will be done." It is still true that we can accomplish things together that cannot be accomplished alone, and this is the hunger of the human heart. Through small groups, mission work, study, and worship, human beings can still grow. Through this common life, taste God's dream for the world. It is in God's dream for our world, the kingdom of God on earth, that our true hope lies. It is still the strongest hope our world has to offer.

But the Advocate, the Holy Spirit, whom the Father will send in my name, will teach you everything, and remind you of everything I have said to you. Peace I leave with you; my peace I give to you. I do not give to you as the world gives. Do not let your hearts be troubled, and do not let them be afraid. (John 14:26-27)

The universal sign of surrender in the modern world is the lone figure with hands up in the air, signaling by the open stance that she or he is not armed and is no threat. Not ironically, this is the same sign of the pastoral benediction, and the same posture of Jesus in paintings throughout the centuries as he takes his final leave from his disciples.

Jesus strode through a dark and dangerous time, completely vulnerable to the world. Rejecting safety and security, he entered Jerusalem so he could be with his people to celebrate Passover. His fearlessness cost him his life. Though his followers initially gathered behind locked doors, they soon took to the streets, opening up houses and homes to all who were hungry and thirsty for the gospel. Though they were repeatedly arrested and often killed, their message spread through the Roman Empire to forge a new kind of empire. Their repeated adaptability to the surrounding culture enabled them to thrive across the world, and the empire of Jesus Christ still survives today, while others may crumble. When we refuse to succumb to our temptations for decline, we will find new life, against which the forces of hell cannot prevail.

Appendix
Leadership Covenant

P reface: As people of faith, we have a longstanding practice of entering covenantal relationships with God and with each other. God initiated the covenant with Abraham, Isaac, and the Israelite people. In Jesus, God established a new covenantal relationship through the cross and resurrection. Members of the early Christian Church organized themselves around spiritual gifts and covenant, recognizing both differing gifts and the need to use those gifts inside a covenant called the church. Covenant, in this sense, means "I share these as highest values" or "I will do my best to live by these standards." In this spirit our Committee on Nominations and Leadership Development offers the following covenant for church leaders:

OUR CORE VALUES

(Taken from *Five Practices for Fruitful Congregations*, by Bishop Robert Schnase)

Practice Radical Hospitality

Worship Faithfully and Passionately

Engage in Ongoing Faith Development Leading to Personal Transformation

Risk-Taking Mission Woven into Personal Life

Practice Extravagant Generosity

Strive for Excellence and Fruitfulness

LEADERSHIP QUALITIES

(Our interpretation of the vows of membership in The United Methodist Church)

As a leader I covenant to:

Place regular worship attendance above all other obligations.

Pray daily for the church's mission and values, asking where God will use me this day.

Financially support the church and God's work through regular tithes, gifts, and offerings in an amount appropriate to being a good steward of the resources God has provided me.

Practice service with God's people each week as a part of my own spiritual development. I will find spiritual growth and fulfillment in growing and spreading our faith to others.

The first four qualities are the vows we all take when we join the church, so they actually are behaviors expected of all church members. When leaders model this behavior, the congregation will take their own vows more seriously as well.

Know the vision, purpose, and journey of the church and embody the core values of the church.

Be responsible not only for doing an excellent job in my own area of service, but also for being a role model and mentor for others.

Hold myself and others accountable for commitments and promises and encourage faithfulness in the completion of tasks as a sign of valuing and caring for others.

Keep the focus of the church's life on the vision, purpose, journey, and core values of the church while believing in God's ongoing power to change lives.

Reinforce the empowering nature of the Church by encouraging others to find new ways to extend and expand the ministry of the Church.

Embrace the need for change consistent with the vision, purpose, and journey of the Church.

Covenant of Respect

Trust in the best intentions of those around you. Seek to understand and provide a positive environment for healthy discussion and conflict.

Be a truth and reconciliation person for whom every meeting, every utterance, every gesture is about truth and reconciliation in the best interest of the Church.

Create in yourself an openness to change as part of God's creation, an opportunity for growth and revelation. Embrace others and create an open and inviting atmosphere for others to participate.

Open your heart and mind to God's love, as incarnate in Jesus, reducing your anxiety and drawing you toward reconciliation and being a reconciler.

Trust that God is present in all parties in the midst of a disagreement. Seek common ground and options to reach consensus.

Provide the same courtesy, respect, and understanding to others as you would have offered to you.

Do not gossip about the church, the members, or its leaders.

Notes

Foreword

1. This quote, used by many authors since the late 1990s, is undocumented and unlikely to have been written by Darwin. See R. D. Norton, "The Changing Information Technology Roles, 1986-1996," in *Regional Science Perspectives in Economic Analysis: A Festschrift in Memory of Benjamin H. Stevens*, ed. Michael L. Lahr and Ronald E. Miller, Contributions to Economic Analysis, 249 (New York: Elsevier, 2001), 251.

2. See Jeff Dyer, Hal Gregersen, and Clayton M. Christensen, *The Innovator's DNA: Mastering the Five Skills of Disruptive Innovators* (Boston: Harvard Business Review Press, 2011), a followup book to Christensen's earlier volume (*The Innovator's Dilemma: When New Technologies Cause Great Firms to Fail* [Boston: Harvard Business School Press, 1997]) that popularized the concept of "disruptive innovation."

3. Winston Churchill, *My Early Life: 1874-1904* (New York: Simon & Schuster, 1996), 110.

4. Quoted in Mike Lopresti, "Ping-Pong Power: China's Slam Dunk," *USA Today*, 19 August 2008, www.usatoday.com/sports/columnist/lopresti/2008-08-18-table-tennis_N.htm.

5. Conrad H. Gempf has written a whole wonderful book on this one fact called *Jesus Asked: What He Wanted to Know* (Grand Rapids: Zondervan, 2003). See also David Dark, *The Sacredness of Questioning Everything* (Grand Rapids: Zondervan, 2009).

6. See, for example, John 5:24 KJV; 6:53 NIV; 8:58 NIV.

7. James Joyce, "A Painful Case," in his *Dubliners: Authoritative Text, Contents, Criticism*, ed. Margot Norris, Hans Walter Gabler, and Walter Hettche (New York: W. W. Norton, 2006), 90.

Preface

1. Benton Johnson, Dean R. Hoge, and Donald A. Luidens, "Mainline Churches: The Real Reason for Decline," *First Things Magazine*, March 1993.

Chapter Six

1. Rendle, Gil, "The Legacy Conversation: Helping a Church Die with Dignity," *Circuit Rider*, February 2011.

Chapter Nine

1. "Welcoming Visitors Is a Long Journey," *Transformation Magazine* 1, no. 2, Desert Southwest Conference, Summer 2010.

2. Ibid.

3. David de Wetter, Ilene Gochman, Rich Luss, Rick Sherwood, "UMC Call to Action: Vital Congregations Research Project, Towers Watson," June 28, 2010.

Part IV

1. David de Wetter, Ilene Gochman, Rich Luss, Rick Sherwood, "UMC Call to Action: Vital Congregations Research Project, Towers Watson," June 28, 2010.